Grief
and
God

When Religion
Does More Harm Than Healing

Dr. Terri Daniel
with Danny Mandel

Grief
and
God

When Religion
Does More Harm Than Healing

Dr. Terri Daniel
with Danny Mandell

© 2019

ISBN-13: 978-0-9623062-0-4

Contents

For Danny

Acknowledgments

Profound thanks to the brilliant psychologists, theologians and chaplains who have shaped my world:

- Marcus Borg, Larry Hansen, John Dominic Crossan, Bart Ehrman, James Fowler, Richard Elliot Friedman, Jose Garcia, Dale Martin, John Shelby Spong

And to the friends and loved ones who have supported me on this journey:

- Lisa Beytia, Robin Clark, Wendy Cobina DeMos, Brant Huddleston, Mary MacDonald-Lewis and Carol Yurick for proofreading and cheerleading

- Stanley Chagala -- for teaching me about The Ancestors

- Don Greenberg -- for vintage yellow dishes and a lifetime of friendship

- Lee Green -- for more than words can describe

- Pamela J. Hunter -- for beautiful book cover design

- Michelle Manley -- for beautiful interior book design

- Spootie Daniel -- for TRUE unconditional love

- Floyd Thompkins -- for believing in my ability to teach

- Robert Woodcox -- for believing in my ability to edit

Introduction

In many religious traditions, God is believed to be responsive to the needs of believers, and in difficult times, believers turn to God for comfort, security and guidance. When God is viewed as a benevolent protector that can shield us from harm in response to prayers or piety, what happens to faith -- and healing -- when God fails to provide that protection?

This book explores the cognitive dissonance we experience when our religious beliefs -- whether inherited or chosen -- do not match up with our lived experience. The content in these pages is based on my 2019 doctoral dissertation entitled *Toxic Theology as a Contributing Factor in Complicated Grief,* a topic inspired by my experiences helping grieving individuals cope with their losses. In that role, as an educator and spiritual caregiver, I offer supportive companionship and healing tools specifically for the grief journey. But I'm also concerned with the psycho-social health of my students and clients *in general.*

Through that lens I've observed certain theological mindsets that can interfere with healing and psychological well-being. I've seen how these mindsets, which tend to be rooted in Judeo-Christian doctrine, can lead to complications in the mourning process, which can result in confusion, depression, and the inability to regain emotional equilibrium. I refer to these views as "toxic theologies," and in this book you will come to understand the definition of that term, and also the definition of "complicated grief." In addition, we'll explore alternative theologies, cosmologies and spiritual practices that can be helpful for those who face this unique challenge.

From an academic perspective, the current body of research contains some excellent material on toxic theology and also on complicated mourning, but very little linking the two together. It is generally agreed that the few studies that do exist in this area yield inconsistent results.[1] Grief researchers have compiled lists of factors that can complicate the mourning process (such as traumatic death, mental illness, death of a child, socially unacceptable death or a lack of social support), but specific religious beliefs are generally not included on those lists.

Current research on the impact of religious belief on loss and grief finds that religious coping can be both helpful *and* harmful. The vagaries of this conclusion are due to the fact that it is so difficult to define religious belief.[2] As an example of how challenging this is for researchers, in their interviews with 678 grievers, Christian, Aoun and Breen acknowledged that their questionnaires didn't provide definitions for religious vs. spiritual beliefs, so they could not know how these constructions were interpreted by the research subjects.[3]

In past decades, the role of religion in one's life was measured in traditional, simplistic terms, such as frequency of church attendance or "belief in God." This doesn't account for millions of people who believe in some form of God but never attend church, nor does it allow for variations in individual concepts of God or a spiritual life that doesn't fit within the parameters of established religious traditions. As Wortman and Park observed, "It has become increasingly clear to researchers that simple global conceptualizations of religion do not adequately capture the complex nature of religion in people's lives."[4]

A favorite professor of mine once said, "When talking about theology, nobody knows what they're talking about." Religious scholars can rely on research and history, but even with those tools, each individual has their own interpretation of the unseen world. We cannot define God any more than we can say that one religion's depiction of the afterlife is more accurate than another's. But we *can* say that some interpretations are more life-affirming, more personally empowering and more healing than others. And nowhere is this more evident than in the lives of grieving or traumatized individuals grappling with a spiritual crisis.

I thank you for your interest in this important topic. I realize that this material is controversial and that some people may find some of it offensive. As a disclaimer of sorts, I offer this: Most of what I say in the following pages is based on personal experience and observation, and you will see my personal opinion coming through at times. However, as an academic, I also made sure to support my position with bona fide research from leading voices in theology and psychology.

If you are struggling with loss and grief -- particularly if religious issues are involved -- it is my sincere hope that you'll find some wisdom and guidance in these pages. If you are a bereavement professional, counselor or member of the clergy, I invite you to explore the tools offered here in search of new perspectives to help your clients and congregants.

Rev. Dr. Terri Daniel
April 2019

A note about references to "The Old Testament" in this book...

In contemporary theological circles, *The Old Testament* is now referred to as *The Hebrew Bible*, to dispel the notion that it has become irrelevant and has been replaced by a "new" testament. Throughout the text, I use "The Hebrew Bible" in all references to The Old Testament.

"It's not that those ancient people told literal stories and we are now smart enough to take them symbolically, but that they told them symbolically, and we are now dumb enough to take them literally."

-- JOHN DOMINIC CROSSAN

1

Did God Throw It Back Down?

In October 2015 a television news crew covered the story of a ten year-old boy named Kyler Bradley, who had recently been diagnosed with inoperable brain cancer. The crew filmed Kyler in his classroom surrounded by his friends, who were instructed by the teacher to "pray for a miracle."

These were the exact words spoken by the on-air reporter in the news segment:

> "Kyler believes in miracles. So do his classmates. Their teacher planted that idea when she told 30 ten year-olds about Kyler's cancer."

The reporter then went on to interview the children, one of whom said, "If everybody prays for him, God will listen."[5]

Kyler died six months later, and when I shared this story with the educators and counselors in my professional network, there was an impassioned discussion about the teacher's inappropriate decision to use prayer as a coping strategy for the students. We wondered how the parents of those children dealt with the inevitable question, "Why didn't God listen?"

Events like this create fertile ground for conflict between religious belief and reality. Not only did those children have to grieve the loss of their friend, they were also forced -- by the teacher's insistence on prayer -- to grapple with complex theological questions.

When we view God as a haven of safety[6] that is responsive to our needs, we may feel abandoned when God fails to insulate us from tragedy. While the image of God as a protector who shields us from harm and a partner with whom we can negotiate may be comforting, what happens to faith and healing when God does not provide the expected protection?

When I was working on my undergrad degree in religious studies, my favorite course was *The Psychology of Religion*. That's where I was introduced to the work of James Fowler, a progressive theologian who analyzed the way we develop our concepts of the divine over the course of the lifespan. In an attempt to understand what Kyler's classmates might have believed about their ability to influence Kyler's fate with prayer, we can begin by looking at James Fowler's research. His pioneering work, *Stages of Faith: The Psychology of Human Development and the Quest for Meaning,* proposed that an individual's concept of God is rooted in the values and beliefs of the child's family and community. But as the child matures, this concept may change to reflect the child's experiences and exposure to new information over the years. Briefly, Fowler identified the following developmental stages in this process:

Stage 0: Primal Faith

The child's view of the world is formed by its relationship with its caregivers. Whether it is a relationship of safety and trust or a relationship of fear and pain, images of "God" begin to form that can influence developing spiritual perceptions.[7]

Stage 1: Intuitive-Projective Faith

Between two and six years of age a child can use words to describe thoughts and experiences. This is also the age when many children are first exposed to religious education, and because logical processes of discernment are not yet fully developed, the child will likely assume that stories are literal truth.[8] In terms of loss and grief, an individual in Stage 1 faith development might believe that a deceased person went up into the sky to live in heaven with a harp and a halo.

Stage 2: Mythic-Literal Faith

As the child's cognitive abilities evolve, while able to recall and re-tell stories, she is not quite able to discern what is mythical and what is literal. This stage is typical in the elementary school years, but Fowler's research shows that adolescents and some adults remain in this stage indefinitely, interpreting symbols and events as literal fact.[9] In terms of loss and grief, a good example can be found in the story of a four-year-old who sees a dead seagull while walking on the beach with his father. The child asks, "What happened to the bird?" The father says, "The bird died and went to heaven." The child looks up to heaven, then down at the bird, and asks, "Did God throw it back down?"[10]

Stage 3: Synthetic-Conventional Faith

In early adolescence, as children begin to explore the social world outside the sphere of their families, anthropomorphic images of God become prominent because they are *personal*, where God becomes a friend and companion who knows the child intimately.[11] In terms of loss and grief, when God is seen as a trusted companion and protector, faith can be shaken when a loss occurs.

Stage 4: Individuative-Reflective Faith

At Stage 4, Fowler says, "The person is pushed out of, or steps out of, the circle of interpersonal relationships that have sustained his life to that point."[12] This may express itself as a "crisis of faith" that causes one to re-examine closely-held beliefs and lifelong allegiances in a quest to attain deeper understanding. In response to loss and grief, the person may feel abandoned by God and unsure where to place faith and trust.

Stage 5: Conjunctive Faith

After the crisis of Stage 4, one becomes "alive to paradox... and understands that truth has many dimensions which have to be held together in paradoxical tension."[13] At this stage, a griever may experience a profound shift in his or her personal theology, and begin to explore new beliefs and cosmologies.

Stage 6: Universalizing Faith

Fowler characterizes Stage 6 as "one in which persons begin radically to live as though what Christians and Jews call the 'kingdom of God' were already a fact."[14] The individual's ego-centered needs and attachments take a back seat to an awareness of oneness with all living things, so that harmony, rather than personal security or protection, becomes a priority.

Fowler points out that many people remain caught between stages three and four,[15] and that some adults even remain at stage two.[16] An example of this range of faith styles can be seen in the following discussion I overheard between three boys (11-14 years old) while facilitating an art therapy group for bereaved adolescents. All three boys had experienced the recent death of a parent:[17]

Matthew: I don't understand how anybody could go to Heaven. There are too many rules. My dad never went to church, and he was an alcoholic, so does that mean he didn't go to Heaven?

Justin: No. He can still go, because God forgives everybody, right? So doesn't that mean everybody will go to Heaven?

Sean: But then there would be too many people there. How could all those people fit up there in the sky?

Another boy in the same group, Taylor, told the story of his mother taking her own life. He'd heard that suicide was a sin, and worried about where she would spend eternity.

Matthew and Justin have a Stage 3 understanding of the afterlife, but they are beginning to notice some contradictions in what they've been taught. Sean, the youngest of the three, is grappling with a Stage 2 literal interpretation of a heaven that is physically located in the sky. If these boys had not just experienced the death of a parent, it is unlikely they would be having a conversation like this. Their losses are triggering questions that can lead to deeper understanding. Hopefully their curiosity will be encouraged at home and in their communities.

Psychologist and theologian Daniel Schipani points out that many of the toxic religious beliefs we recognize today are rooted in the Abrahamic faith traditions. He identifies some of their key features:[18]

- They include forms of emotional, spiritual, moral and sometimes physical or sexual violence and power abuse.

- They compromise emotional/mental health and are connected to mental/emotional dysfunction.

- They exist on a spectrum of intensity ranging from unhealthy to harmful to lethal.

Although the examples of the children given above do not constitute abuse or necessarily lead to mental dysfunction, they could easily fit into the "unhealthy" end of Schipani's spectrum, depending on how the children's questions were answered by their families, churches or teachers. If Matthew's evangelical grandmother insisted that his father didn't go to heaven because he wasn't saved, or if someone told Taylor that his mother went to hell for suicide, the seeds of toxic theology would be firmly planted in the fertile soil of a profound loss.

Schipani also reminds us that the psychological self is always engaged along with the spiritual self, and both psychology and theology must be considered when offering spiritual care to others, or when working on our own personal spiritual growth. Religious beliefs, influences and indoctrinations cannot -- and should not -- be separated from psychology when working with loss, trauma and grief. The impact of religious belief is enormous, and while it can be helpful and theologically sound for some people, it is just as likely to be dangerous and psychologically dysfunctional for others.[19]

Defining Toxic Theology

The first time I heard the term "bad theology" was in graduate school after a debate with a very conservative professor. It was at Fordham University in the Pastoral Care and Counseling program, and the professor was a Catholic priest, as were many faculty members in the Religious Studies department at Fordham.

I had written an essay about the concept of "universalism," which as I understand it, means that the spiritual world (or the presence of God, or a relationship with the divine, or whatever you want to call it) is everywhere, and is part of everything. It is available to everybody, open to an infinite number of interpretations and forms, and is not defined by any particular doctrine, belief system or religious tradition. It is *inclusive* rather than *exclusive*.

The professor did not like my perspective at all. He gave me a B- on the paper and a B in the class (laying waste to my 4.0 GPA). His only feedback on my essay was this stunningly absurd comment:

> "The problem with a universal idea of God is that it cannot be proven rationally, and it leaves adherents to rely on belief alone."

I read his words several times to make sure I was reading them correctly. Was he actually saying that the test of good theology is that it can be "proven rationally?" And that religious adherence shouldn't rely on "belief alone?" It made no sense that a committed Catholic would say such a thing, since Catholicism is based almost entirely on stories that can't be proven rationally, and *requires* adherents to rely on belief alone. How could he not see the glaring contradiction here?

I was so disturbed by the professor's response that I called on several knowledgeable friends to help me make sense of his ridiculous argument. One such friend was an academic advisor of mine named Bill, who also happens to be a former Catholic priest (he left the priesthood so he could marry).

"Your professor is practicing bad theology," Bill said.

After that I began hearing the term *bad theology* wherever I went, and it wasn't long before it morphed into *toxic theology*, catching the pop culture wave that labeled all kinds of negative experiences as *toxic* (toxic relationships, toxic parents, toxic culture, toxic people, toxic masculinity, etc.). The term "toxic theology" has now officially entered the cultural lexicon. And not a moment too soon.

Schipani tells us that the process of inner (spiritual) healing should always produce a positive effect on mental and emotional health.[20] He defines *toxic theology* as any system that undermines emotional/mental health and includes forms of emotional, mental or spiritual violence. He identifies these characteristics:[21]

- Expresses itself in terms of beliefs, attitudes/relationships and practices with different degrees of toxicity.

- Includes a measure of violence (a form of power or abuse that harms or injures self and/others). Such violence is always emotional, spiritual/moral, and sometimes physical (including sexual violence).

- Uniquely compromises the whole self; spiritual, mental/emotional and physical dimensions.

- Undermines emotional/mental health (no exceptions!).

- Directly connected with mental/emotional dysfunction.

- Mental/emotional dysfunction affects inner experience and outward manifestation of spirituality.

- "Hamster wheel syndrome" (running in circles).

- Often directly connected to religion (esp. in terms of convictions, practices, and supporting theologies).

- Abrahamic faith traditions appear to supply particular "content" to toxic spiritualities (example, interpretation of scripture, notions of the divine, etc.)

- Non-religious spiritualities can also be(come) toxic.[22]

Schipani says that although not all toxic spirituality is fundamentalist, all forms of fundamentalism sustain some form of toxic theology because they debilitate the human spirit. This is accomplished through policies that suppress critical thinking and forbid questioning, regard anyone outside the group with suspicion, and promote a vision of the future that requires the conversion of outsiders.[23]

Psychologist David Benner, who studies religious psychodynamics, says that theology is toxic when it limits spiritual experience to merely accepting beliefs and doctrines.[24] Similarly, researchers Tarico and Winell, in their paper on *The Sad, Twisted Truth about Conservative Christianity's Effect on the Mind*, find that the key attributes of toxic theology include:[25]

- An authoritarian power hierarchy that demands obedience.
- Policies of separatism.
- Restricted access to outside sources of information.
- A threat-based reality (hell, divine punishment, catastrophic end times).
- Psychological mind-control techniques that encourage isolation.

And here's my own list of features found in toxic theologies:

- Followers are held to a rigid, unyielding system of beliefs.
- Questioning and exploration is discouraged.
- Outsiders are viewed with suspicion or disdain.
- Religious pluralism is unacceptable.
- Biblical texts are interpreted literally.
- God is seen as an authoritarian parental figure.
- A belief that God rewards piety and faithfulness.

- Behaviors/ beliefs not in line with strict doctrines are punished by God.

- Natural disasters, epidemics and community tragedies are curses from God.

While many of the above-mentioned definitions seem to point specifically to Judeo-Christian dogmas, even within conservative Christian circles there are discussions about toxic theology. A page on the website for the evangelical *700 Club* lists "Signs of Toxic Religion" that echo some of the characteristics described above, attributing these qualities to the poisoning of the established church by an infusion of what they call "dangerous thinking."[26] Their list condemns those who hold self-righteous views and refuse to embrace change. But they are looking into a mirror, because their own form of toxic theology meets all the above criteria, and even disparages other Christians who don't interpret Christianity the same way they do.

As an amusing (but sad) example of this group's aversion to religious pluralism, 700 Club founder Pat Robertson has publicly stated that practicing yoga is dangerous for Christians because it "tricks people into speaking in Hindu and praying to a Hindu deity."[27] Robertson's stance against yoga is supported by many Christian extremists, among them, a woman named Laurette Willis, who believes that the "New Age lifestyle" (and yoga in particular) is fraught with spiritual pitfalls.[28] To address the growing popularity of these practices, Laurette created a program called *Praise Moves* as a Christian alternative to yoga.[29] Even though she uses all the traditional yoga postures (but sanctifies them by re-naming them after scripture passages), she believes that yoga postures are offerings to Hindu gods, which are false idols. She explains that

Christians don't avoid yoga out of fear, but out of wisdom and out of love for those who are "not as spiritually mature as we are."[30]

Her ideas qualify as an expression of toxic theology on multiple counts, including policies of separatism, restricted access to outside sources of information, and limiting spiritual experience to merely accepting beliefs and doctrines. For a Christian who finds yoga to be relaxing and beneficial to health, this presents a spiritual dilemma that can result in feelings of confusion and guilt.

I spend a lot of time on road trips, driving to speaking engagements around the country. I often listen to Christian radio stations along the way, because they fascinate me, especially the ones that provide on-air counseling to callers. One call I will never forget came from a man who said he'd been reading about near-death and out-of-body experiences and found the topic of great interest. He was calling to ask if it was OK for him to explore this. He literally asked the radio show host, "What should I believe?" The host answered, "If it's not in scripture, then you should not pay any attention to it. It's Satan trying to turn you away from Christ."

The fact is, these types of experiences are found throughout scripture, and were also an important element in the lives of the saints and early Christian mystics. But that's another story.

Attachment Theory and Images of God

In the modern Western world, God is usually referred to as a *person*, specifically, a male person addressed as "father." In the realm of psychology -- in object-relations theory -- the person known as God could be considered an *illusory transitional object* that is modeled on a child's relationship with its parents and the attachments experienced in those relationships.[31]

In order to understand how children develop these attachments, we begin with Bowlby's foundational research on attachment behavior, which he defines as "seeking and maintaining proximity to another individual."[32] In early childhood, that individual is usually a parent or caregiver, which Bowlby refers to as the "attachment figure" (AF). As long as the family environment is stable, a child's secure relationship with the AF will remain in place throughout the subsequent years of the child's development.[33]

Referring back to Fowler's stages of faith, in the process of faith development, the AF would be an anthropomorphized (humanized) image of God. With God as the AF, as long as God is providing protection and nurturing, the attachment remains secure. But when the assumption of protection is challenged by the interference of loss or trauma, the secure attachment is threatened.

Freud described our formation of the western god image as based on our need for an exalted father figure. But a father image is not necessarily helpful, especially for individuals who have not experienced supportive fathers during their lifetime. In the words of Jewish mystic Rabbi David Cooper, "As long as we relate to God as father and we as children, we sustain the dysfunctional paternalistic model in which father knows best. We not only remain alienated with a sense of abandonment, we relinquish our personal sense of responsibility."[34]

When traumatized persons cling to the childhood image of God as parent/protector, they might focus their energy on being angry at God for failing to provide the expected protection, rather than on the inner resources necessary for resilience and healing. If they also see God as a harsh judge and punisher, the anger may mix with guilt and fear, further inhibiting the healing process. In Chapter Four we will see several examples of this.

Dr. Christopher Ellison, whose research focuses on the implications of religion and spirituality for mental and physical health, notes that "the portrait of God as a parental attachment figure is highly compatible with the beliefs of Christianity, and indeed, with many of the major world religions, in which God is commonly depicted as a loving God who is responsive to the needs of believers."[35] He describes how a believer may seek proximity to God in difficult times as a source of safety and strength for facing challenges. But while this secure attachment may provide comfort during stressful times based on a relationship of love and security, believers can also experience an anxious or insecure attachment that exacerbates stress when the relationship is inconsistent and confusing.[36]

Children raised with a "protector/punisher" image of God often embrace that image for a lifetime without critical investigation. These images are supported by community and culture as children mature into adulthood. Some individuals will move through evolving stages of spiritual development, but for others, the childhood images are so deeply ingrained that they are not questioned until an existential crisis -- usually triggered by a profound trauma or loss -- prompts re-examination.

Brite Divinity School professors Howard Stone and James Duke[37] give us an example of how some adults accept childhood imagery without hesitation, and are uncomfortable with deeper exploration. In their book, *How to Think Theologically*, they asked a group of church parishioners to define their church's theology. The parishioners responded with comments that sounded like they were uttered by children, such as, "God loves us if we go to church and worship," and "The church is where we meet with Jesus."

Stone and Duke observed that many Christians believe what they are taught unquestioningly because they don't feel they are equipped to think as theologians.[38] Believers are often discouraged from theological reflection, even when their beliefs are fraught with contradictions and inadequacies.[39] In addition to the idea that questioning is a threat to faith, Stone and Duke also report that some Christians resist thinking theologically because they "don't understand big words," or feel that studying theology "is only for professors," or "theology has nothing to do with God."[40] But without critical study and exploration, adults who remain engaged with a childhood image of God will often lack the spiritual and emotional tools required by an adult crisis, which can compromise their ability to process loss in a healthy way.

When faced with loss and trauma, it is often necessary to deconstruct the god-as-protective-parent theology in order to make room for a more spacious form of spirituality. Stone and Duke give the example of parents whose toddler falls into their pool and drowns.[41] The anguished parents call out to God, "Why did you let this happen? Why not let *me* die instead?" Relying on their *embedded theology* (faith as described by the church and accepted by its members),[42] the grieving parents are unprepared to negotiate the conflict between their misfortune and their belief that God is good. For some believers, when the crisis abates and recovery begins, the conflict may fade into the background, forgotten for the moment. But for others, it becomes a catalyst for deeper inquiry, and the process of *deliberative theology* (thinking and analyzing rather than just accepting established teachings) can begin.

God or Godzilla?

One of our most toxic ancient concepts is the idea that God demands flawless, inerrant obedience and creates catastrophic punishment whenever that standard is violated. In Chapter 3 we'll ponder what might have been present in the psychology of the Hebrew Bible authors that caused them to write a history based on a God who behaved more like Godzilla than a loving parent. But for now, let's start by looking at the relationship between *myth* and *meaning*.

Mythical stories have immeasurable value in creating societies and theological frameworks, because they establish culture, unified belief systems, community moral codes and collective thinking. But their value can only be realized by working with these stories as metaphors rather than facts. Viewed metaphorically, a culture's stories, myths and legends provide wisdom and personal relevance that can be easily missed when interpreting the stories as literal events, which often contradict each other and do not align with actual history. This is why it is so important to look at religious stories through the lens of critical, historical inquiry rather than through the limited scope of literalism. As Canadian biblical scholar and Anglican priest Tom Harpur astutely pointed out, literalism deprives us of the deeper meanings in these stories by providing a one-dimensional view of concepts that have the potential for multiple levels of understanding.[43]

Many of today's religious beliefs, practices and political alignments are based on ancient mythology that has no historical basis, yet the practices and social structures have endured for centuries. Even a cursory glance at Google search results for "Did the biblical exodus really happen?" reveals a clear division between historical and devotional perspectives. Most in favor of the Exodus story as actual history are religious websites that quote bible passages as evidence, while those opposed tend to be scholarly websites that cite academic research in biblical archeology.

Most American children who were raised with Judeo-Christian theology were told stories about God, creation, the Ten Commandments, heaven and hell, Jesus, Moses, the Bible, Hanukkah, Santa Claus or some combination of the above. Based on those childhood teachings, some of us may have gotten the impression that God is frequently angry and disappointed in humanity because we are unworthy, sinful, marred and imperfect, and can't live up to his expectations. A God who *literally* wipes out the world with a flood, murders those who don't follow his rules and incites genocide against the inhabitants of land he claims for his chosen people presents a frightening picture. Many who were raised with strict religious backgrounds grew up with the "fear of God" and a sense that they are constantly being watched and judged rather than loved and supported.

With this belief as a childhood foundation, some people struggle all their lives to get back into God's good graces in the hope of experiencing God's love and/or being allowed into Heaven. Others reject the idea of spirituality all together. In either case, the true value of the Bible's allegorical teachings is lost.[44]

As I wrote in my 2014 book, *Turning the Corner on Grief Street*:

> "The fear-based view of God that many embrace today was personified in the legendary sermon by Christian theologian Jonathan Edwards in 1741 entitled, *Sinners in the Hands of an Angry God*. Edwards presented hell as a real, physical location, and promised an eternity of punishment for all who do not embrace Christ, and

specifically cited scripture that expresses God's wrath at the "wicked unbelieving Israelites" who deserve "infinite punishment" for their sins.[45]

"The god described in these scenarios presents a baffling contradiction. On the one hand he is a 'matchless paragon of virtue' which humans are required to revere and emulate in blind faith,[46] but he also appears to be, equally, a violent psychopath prone to irrational rages, racial bigotry and mass murder, with mood swings that could be compared to bi-polar disorder. As Helsel describes, attempts to understand or worship such a god has often required a sacrifice of the intellect.[47]

"In her article, *A Beautiful Anger*, which appears in a fundamentalist Christian publication, author Linda Falter acknowledges that the terrifying aspects of God's behavior are in fact part of God's nature, along with his other human attributes, such as eyes and nostrils.[48] She even compares God's actions to her own actions as a parent, and wonders why humans created a god with this type of personality. But rather than pursue this question with intellectual curiosity and psychological insight, she simply concludes that God's behavior is 'beyond our pay grade to judge,' since God's anger is different than ours because it has a holier purpose.[49]

"This is an example of the unquestioning allegiance to the anthropomorphic idea of God to which so many Jews, Christians and Muslims subscribe. Rather than analyzing the behavior of the mythical entity written about by the ancients, and identifying the reasons why that entity's behavior so accurately reflects our own, Falter, like millions of other believers, simply shrugs it off as a mystery that we are not worthy to comprehend. And here we find the core of one of theology's greatest questions: How could God's anger be different than ours if we created the idea of this angry God in the first place?"

2

Toxic Theology on the Public Stage

In November 2018 my home state of California experienced the worst wildfire in its recorded history, which destroyed an entire town, burning 16,000 structures and killing 86 people.[50] In his article, *Is California Under a Curse?* Gerald Flurry, pastor of the biblically-orthodox Philadelphia Church of God, had this to say about those fires:

> "God does punish us with 'natural' disasters. 'Thou shalt be visited of the Lord of hosts with thunder, and with earthquake, and great noise, with storm and tempest, and the flame of devouring fire' (Isaiah 29:6). God says He visits, or punishes, us with the flame of devouring fire... The sooner we repent, the sooner the curses will end."[51]

Former child actor and outspoken evangelical Kirk Cameron, after Hurricanes Irma and Harvey in 2017, went on Facebook to proclaim that these events were sent by God so human beings could repent.[52] And in response to Hurricane Sandy in 2012, conservative Christian pastor John McTernan told his followers that God is destroying America in response to "the homosexual agenda."[53]

Professor of religious history Matthew Schmalz, in a blog post dispelling the belief that natural disasters are curses from God, cites all the usual examples from scripture of why so many people believe this. But as a scholar who relies on historical/critical analysis, he also looks to other sources, including the Epistle of James, which says that God does *not* test or tempt us, but rewards us for enduring difficult times. He also interprets the writings of early Christian philosopher Origen as teaching that suffering is a path to self-knowledge and to a deeper connection to God. In these views, Schmalz says, suffering is not inflicted as punishment from God, but as something that can actually bring us closer to God and to one another. Believing that God punishes us with hurricanes, floods and earthquakes, Schmalz says, "reduces the divine to human terms."[54]

Returning to our focus on the impact of toxic theology on grief, one of the last places one might expect to find a theology of punishment would be in a grief support group. Yet the website for the Christian grief support group *Grief Share* offers this distressing explanation for the pain that grievers experience:[55]

GOD'S PLAN TO END YOUR SUFFERING

Not only does God want to ease your suffering, He actually relates to it. How can God understand a human problem like grief? He can relate because He grieved the unjust execution of His Son, Jesus. As painful as it was, God allowed Jesus to die as part of His plan to end suffering and death. He wanted to bring comfort, hope, and healing to you. But to appreciate this plan, you have to understand the reason suffering and death exist.

THE REASON WE SUFFER

All of us have disobeyed God. This is not a new problem. It stretches all the way back to Adam and Eve. The Bible calls this disobedience "sin," and describes its ultimate consequence:

> "All have sinned and fall short of the glory of God." (Romans 3:23)

> "The wages of sin is death." (Romans 6:23a)

THIS CREATES A SEEMINGLY HOPELESS FUTURE FOR US:

- Because God is pure and holy, He cannot tolerate sin.

- He punishes sin. It's the only possible response consistent with His righteous character.

- The penalty for our sin is suffering in this life and physical death followed by eternal punishment.

After delivering this alarming message, the website offers "hope for healing" by assuring its site visitors (and thousands of group members worldwide) that "God's love and mercy are so deep that He wants to rescue each of us from the consequences of our disobedience (sin)."[56]

When individuals feel that they are under constant supervision by a patriarchal god who punishes them for disobedience or wrongdoing, it can create feelings of powerlessness, unworthiness and shame.[57] Stephen Pattison, a professor of religion and ethics, has done extensive research on individual and family shame. He observes that Christianity "has failed to recognize the way in which its own ideology and practices may have contributed to the products and exploitation of dysfunctional shame."[58] He also states that doctrines of salvation and atonement, while capable of offering healing and hope, are equally capable of producing guilt and shame.[59] For a grieving mother who just lost a teenage son to suicide, or a husband who feels he didn't provide adequate care for his ailing wife before she died, messages like Grief Share's can be soul-crushing.

William Morrow, in *Toxic Religion and the Daughters of Job,* defines toxic religion as any system in which legitimate human experiences and responses are shamed by religious institutions and systems. Psychological disruption can emerge when a person's perception of the beliefs and behaviors required by their religion are in conflict with the person's actual lived experience.[60]

Morrow goes on to say, "To feel shame is to be seen in a diminished sense," and notes that the monotheistic faith of ancient Israel contains shaming potential.[61] In a shaming relationship, one party has power over another, and when that power is over-used or abused, as in the case of over-controlling religious systems, it can cause psychological injury.[62] He specifically identifies "perfectionist-retributionist doctrines"-- in which natural human experience does not match up with the moral requirements of a demanding religious doctrine -- as an expression of toxic religion.[63]

One of the most extreme examples of toxic theology can be seen in the Westboro Baptist church, founded by the late Fred Phelps, creator of the "God Hates Fags" movement. Phelps' son Nathan, who left the church as an adult along with several other members who were raised in the church, spent his childhood protesting in public with other children, carrying signs that said, "God Hates You" and "Soldiers Die, God Laughs." This group was notorious for, among other things, protesting at military funerals, claiming that the fallen soldiers died as the result of America's tolerance for gay people in the military. In his TED talk,[64] Nathan describes what it's like for a child's worldview and sense of morality to be formed in an atmosphere of hate and terror in the name of God. He recounts the pain of growing up filled with fear and self-doubt while he struggled with the image of an angry, hateful god, and now teaches others how to recognize dangerous cults.

Most American children grow up with beautiful images of God and religious life. Many of us were raised on greeting card depictions of adorable children kneeling at their bedtime prayers, saying grace at the family dinner table or bathed in ethereal light as they walk hand-in-hand with Jesus. This iconic imagery invites children to see the spiritual world as a safe, magical space where they will be loved and cared for.

But for children raised like Nathan Phelps was, or in any environment where children are taught to live in fear of God's wrath, the world of faith and religion is far from safe. For some, it is a place of terror, intimidation and abuse. While some children are taught to see themselves as beloved children of God, others are raised with horror movie imagery inspired by Jonathan Edwards', *Sinners in the Hands of an Angry God*. According to Edwards, all of humanity is dangling over glowing flames in the pit of hell, controlled by a god that "abhors" us, and sees us as "worthy of nothing more than to be cast to the fire."[65]

Janet Heimlich, in her book *Breaking Their Will*, explores how religion can often function as an authoritarian culture that creates terror among followers. She identifies characteristics in religious authoritarian systems that include literal interpretation of scripture as the source of absolute rule, and the threat of punishment for non-conformity. Children raised in this ethos fail to develop critical thinking skills and intellectual autonomy. They can grow up projecting their fear of God onto the world at large, perceiving everything outside the immediate religious community as dangerous, evil and suspicious.

A random search through Christian internet sites turns up countless frightening perspectives on suffering that are guaranteed to make the tasks of grieving more challenging. We'll look more into our relationship with suffering in Chapter 3, but relative to our exploration of bad theology in this chapter, here's an example of a quintessentially toxic statement:

> "Disease, of course, is another major cause of suffering. The reasons for illnesses are too numerous to list. However, God promised the ancient Israelites that, if they diligently observed His instructions, which included dietary, sanitation and agricultural laws, He would not afflict them with the diseases He had brought on the Egyptians (Exodus 15:26). He warned them, however, that ignoring His guidance would result in sickness and disease (Deuteronomy 28:58-61). Controlling disease, then, can relate to whether we listen to God's advice and follow it."[66]

Does this mean that those who follow the dietary laws of the ancient Israelites will never get diseases? Or does it mean that we experience sickness because we don't "listen to God's advice" in general? What is God's advice, exactly? What about children who get sick? Did they ignore God's advice, or is their illness a punishment for the disobedience of their parents?

When I was a hospital chaplain, I visited with devout Christians every day who were afflicted with terrible diseases. Many of them felt they were being punished because they'd disobeyed God in some way, even though they'd been faithful and obedient, and they struggled to understand what they'd done to deserve illness. After listening to hundreds of people who anguished over this question, it seemed to me that they had only two options... either spend a lot of time wondering what they did wrong, or consider the possibility that their religious teachings were wrong.

In the quest for new theologies, millions of people have found a home in "New Age" concepts and practices, which began as an interest in Hindu and Buddhist teachings, but grew into a massive commercial movement that offered an escape from tired old doctrines and dogmas. Like all emerging religious movements, the core foundational ideas may be beautiful and truly spiritual, but over time, in the hands of the marketing machine, the original message gets lost and is simply replaced with new doctrines and dogmas.

In 2006, a documentary film called *The Secret* claimed to reveal the great mysteries of the universe, and the accompanying book became a worldwide best-seller. The message of The Secret was that we could create everything we desire -- wealth, love, happiness, health, and prosperity in all areas of our lives -- by thinking only positive thoughts and speaking only positive words. By contrast, if we think the "wrong" thoughts, we will be broadcasting negative energy, and the universe will respond by giving us negative experiences, such as illness, poverty and loneliness. They called this "the law of attraction."

In the last two decades since the book and film were published, dozens of people have told me stories like this one (from a woman I'll call Becky):

> "I'm a very spiritual person. I do everything I can to stay in a positive manifestation mindset, because I know that my thoughts create my reality. I say affirmations every day, and when negative thoughts appear, I replace them with positive ones. I focus on knowing that I deserve love, health and money. But I'm still poor, and no matter what I do, I'm not able to create money. Not only that, my boyfriend just left me, and my car broke down. I can't afford to fix the car, and I can't pay my rent this month. I'm obviously not manifesting very well. What am I doing wrong?"

The stars of the film are showcased in their million-dollar houses with expensive cars parked in their driveways. They talk about how easy it was for them to acquire these things, thanks to the principles of The Secret, and they even speak about a *spiritual elite,* referring to "the few people living today who actually know The Secret."

Like Becky, millions of people bought into the idea that we could have everything we want by visualizing our dreams coming true and supporting those visions with positive thoughts and affirmations. The essential message is if you're sick, poor or lonely, you're not thinking correctly. If you don't get what you want, you are putting negative energy out into the universe, and attracting negative experiences in return.

This is a simplified explanation of it of course, but it's relevant here because it is no different than many other religious conventions. The judgmental, condemning language in this doctrine divides humanity into those who are succeeding and those who are not (saved vs. unsaved). It doesn't account for the varieties of human experience and the necessity of *balance* in that experience, and also doesn't consider the billions of people on earth who live in poverty, including the 22,000 children who die *every day* due to poverty.[67] Is this because they don't know The Secret?

This kind of thinking shames Becky into feeling that she's on the outside; she's not part of the spiritual elite. Can you see the similarity between Becky's dilemma and the concerns of the Christians in the hospital? Becky practiced her "religion" faithfully, yet she did not receive the promised rewards. Becky has to *prove* that she's faithful by showing the collateral of health, wealth and a happy romantic relationship. Without it, she experiences the same sense of guilt and inadequacy promoted by doctrines of sin and salvation. It's the same old toxic theology re-packaged for a new audience.

Here are some choice toxic teachings from the philosophy of The Secret:

- "The small percentage of people who control all the money in the world are part of a select group of people who know the secret."[68]

- "The Secret gives you everything you want, happiness, health and wealth."[69]

- "Before you begin to embark on the incredible journey towards true enlightenment in the Law of Attraction, it is important that you understand that you can apply it to your life and it can be effective if the correct tools are used."[70]

- "Visualizing that you have received a check for an extraordinary amount of money is a powerful way to send your subconscious mind a new belief that you are earning the kind of money you desire to earn. The secret is to use the check we have provided on this page, to print it up and make it out for the sum of money you desire. Click Here to Print Your Check from The Universe to Attract More Money."[71]

It's easy to see why this caught on. It's just as easy to see that this is nothing more than the old god-in-the-sky theology telling us that if we do a certain thing (say the right prayers, think the right thoughts, join the right group), we won't suffer. What is so damaging about this -- and other teachings that promise special status and freedom from normal human woes -- is that it's based on the idea that suffering is bad and should be avoided.

In the Abrahamic tradition, suffering is often seen as either a punishment for sin or a mysterious, incomprehensible force that is beyond our ability to understand. The leading proponents of the law of attraction seem to think that suffering is unnecessary and can be eliminated by envisioning a world in which everything is exactly the way we want it to be. By contrast, in Buddhism for example, suffering is understood as a necessary part of the soul's accumulation of experience on the journey toward higher awareness.

Human beings cannot live on good experiences alone. Buddhist nun Pema Chodron describes it this way:

> "We always want to get rid of misery rather than see how it works with joy... Inspiration and wretchedness complement each other... With only inspiration we become arrogant. With only wretchedness, we lose our vision."[72]

The point is that suffering has a purpose and *cannot* be avoided. It is a natural part of a balanced incarnate experience; both good and bad experiences are necessary to create a full circuit, like positive and negative charges on a battery. To think otherwise is to have a dysfunctional relationship with suffering.

A DYSFUNCTIONAL RELATIONSHIP WITH SUFFERING:

- We see suffering as punishment
- We see suffering as random and meaningless
- We assume that all suffering is bad
- We scramble desperately to avoid or relieve it
- We cannot sit with anxiety and uncertainty

A HEALTHY RELATIONSHIP WITH SUFFERING:

- We focus on working with suffering rather than trying to stop it.
- We see suffering as a gift of grace that awakens us
- We understand that reassurance devalues suffering
- We see suffering as imbued with meaning and growth
- We strive to be ventilated *in* our suffering rather than insulated *from* it

Positive and Negative Religious Coping

Much of contemporary research on religious coping for dealing with loss is anchored in the work of Dr. Kenneth Pargament and his team in developing the RCOPE (Religious Coping) scale.[73] The scale functions as a measuring tool that can assess a wide range of religious coping mechanisms used by people facing extreme stress, difficulty or loss. The scale addresses both helpful and harmful religious coping mechanisms, which are identified in relation to five basic religious functions:

- Finding meaning in a traumatic or difficult event
- Establishing a sense of control
- Finding comfort in a dangerous world
- A sense of social intimacy and community
- Assistance in major life transitions

The RCOPE scale was designed to provide deeper insight into religious coping behaviors, beyond traditional measures of religiousness, which are usually limited to frequency of prayer or attendance at religious services.[74]

Pargament's Illustrative Methods of Religious Coping [75]

Benevolent Religious Reappraisal	Redefining the stressor through religion as benevolent and potentially beneficial.
Punishing God Reappraisal	Redefining the stressor as a punishment from God for the individual's sins.

Demonic Reappraisal	Redefining the stressor as the act of the Devil.
Reappraisal of God's Powers	Redefining God's powers to influence the stressful situation.
Collaborative Religious Coping	Seeking control through a partnership with God in problem solving.
Deferring Religious Coping	Passively waiting for God to control the situation.
Self-Directing Religious Coping	Seeking control through individual initiative rather than help from God.
Religious Focus	Seeking relief from the stressor through a focus on religion.
Seeking Spiritual Support	Searching for comfort and reassurance through God's love and care.
Religious Purification	Searching for spiritual cleansing through religious actions.
Spiritual Connection	Seeking a sense of connectedness with transcendent forces.
Spiritual Discontent	Expressions of confusion and dissatisfaction with God.

Seeking Support from Clergy or Congregation	Searching for comfort and reassurance through the love and care of congregation members and clergy.
Religious Helping	Attempting to provide spiritual support and comfort to others.
Interpersonal Religious Discontent	Expressions of confusion and dissatisfaction with clergy or congregation.
Religious Forgiving	Looking to religion for help in letting go of anger, hurt, and fear associated with an offense.

The research showed that a belief in divine punishment or demonic intervention as the cause of tragedy is a form of "negative religious coping" that can be associated with decreased mental health outcomes. While many of the research subjects used these negative mechanisms, the majority found comfort and hope (rather than punishment and shame) in their relationship to God when facing trauma or loss.[76] For the most part, people's religious outlooks showed a secure relationship with God. But Pargament also noted that although negative coping strategies were used less often, they expressed a "different religious orientation; one involving a tenuous relationship with God, spiritual struggle, and a threatening view of the world."[77]

While comfort and hope may be the most common response, in my experience working with the bereaved, I have encountered countless cases where specific religious beliefs have exacerbated stress and anxiety, keeping the griever in a state of chronic sadness, guilt and worry. Although such cases may be in the minority, this phenomenon is worthy of study, and investigation into this topic can be of value to counselors, therapists, clergy and clinicians.

Pargament's team came to a similar conclusion:

> "Generally, the positive religious coping pattern was tied to benevolent outcomes, including fewer symptoms of psychological distress, reports of psychological and spiritual growth as a result of the stressor, and interviewer ratings of greater cooperativeness. In contrast, the negative religious coping pattern was associated with signs of emotional distress, such as depression, poorer quality of life, psychological symptoms, and callousness towards others. Religion, these findings suggest, can be a source of distress as well as a source of solutions in coping."[78]

Beliefs and Practices That Can Complicate the Grief Journey

In the previous sections we've covered beliefs such as divine punishment and the image of God as a protective parent, and in this section we'll explore some additional beliefs that can cause confusion, anxiety, depression and even illness for the traumatized and bereaved. While some of the examples given throughout this book might be considered extreme, the examples below are from average people who struggled with toxic beliefs as they worked through their grief (some of these examples will be explored in more detail in the case vignettes in Chapter 4):

- One mother believed that her nine year-old child died from leukemia because God was punishing her for having an abortion 20 years earlier.

- A mother who'd lost all four of her children in separate, unrelated incidents said, "I thought nothing like this would happen to me if I was a good person and pleased God."

- A young wife whose husband was killed by a drunk driver struggled to suppress her anger because she believed that anger comes from Satan and must be resisted.

- A mother whose son died from suicide was plagued with fear that her son would spend eternity in hell.

- Religious friends and family members at the bedside of a dying loved one feared that the person would go to hell if not "saved" before death.

- A dying man in his 50s who'd engaged in criminal activity in his youth had recently become a Christian. But now, facing death, he wondered if his terminal diagnosis at such a young age was a punishment from God, and worried that despite his faith, he may still go to hell for his crimes.

All of these responses are in the realm of negative religious coping styles identified in Pargament's RCOPE scale.

Pattison points out that there are factors inherent in Christian thinking that can produce and prolong a sense of shame by claiming that certain doctrines and behavior codes are the will of God. The paradox is that Christianity can not only instill shame (through doctrines of sin, guilt and unworthiness), but also has the capacity to relieve it (through doctrines of salvation and redemption).[79] In cases of grief that have become complicated by toxic religious beliefs, this paradox can become an even bigger challenge when the griever feels that he is already "saved," and therefore should not deserve punishment.

Melissa Kelly, an associate professor of pastoral care and counseling at Boston College School of Theology, finds that the conflict between doctrine and actual lived experience can be a tremendous stumbling block when navigating loss and bereavement. In her book, *Grief: Contemporary Theory and the Practice of Ministry*, she shares the following case examples:[80]

Corinne

Corrinne grew up going to church every weekend with her aunt. She heard about God's love, but also heard about sin and God's judgment, which made God seem unpredictable, and she wondered how to "keep God happy." At the age of eight, her mother moved away to live with a boyfriend, and although Corinne visited her mother on weekends, she was devastated by the abandonment. When Corinne was in college, her mother died of cancer, despite Corinne's fervent prayers for God to save her.

Corinne prayed to God every night from childhood into adulthood, but now, since God had not only allowed her to be abandoned by her mother, but did not heal her mother's cancer, she worries that God is punishing and abandoning rather than loving and protective.[81]

Robert

Robert and his wife were devastated when their three month-old daughter died, and they turned to their friends, family, and church for support. Robert was pursuing a divinity degree and eventual ordination at the time, but when he discovered that the theology of his tradition did not offer adequate comfort or guidance in the face of this tragedy, he had a crisis of faith. For many months, all he could do was pray the psalms of lament and rail against God.[82]

Angie

After her four year-old son Tyler died suddenly, Angie sought the comfort of God's presence. But there was no comfort to be found, and she felt abandoned. She didn't understand how God, who was a parent himself, could not save her from the worst loss a parent could experience. If Jesus loved little children, how could he let her child die? When friends offered platitudes such as "God must have needed another angel in heaven," or "God never gives us more than we can handle," she wondered if God had done this for a purpose. And when another friend suggested that God was trying to teach her something, she interpreted it to mean that she hadn't been faithful enough, and wondered if God was punishing her for that. Or worse, had God punished Tyler for *her* failings? [83]

David

David believed that God rewards the faithful. He recalls hearing, as a child, "God helps those who help themselves," and "Ask and it shall be given to you." He married, had children and created a beautiful life for his family. He prayed regularly at home and at church for health and happiness.[84]

At age 50, his wife Janet was diagnosed with cancer. With the help of aggressive treatment and the prayers of their church community, the cancer went into remission. David and Janet happily made plans to build their dream house, to enjoy their grandchildren and to retire comfortably, but at 58, Janet's cancer returned, and she died just before Christmas.

David is struggling to figure out where God has been through all this. He believed that God helps those who help themselves, and also believed that his hard work and heartfelt prayers should have been enough for God to step in and "do his part" to save Janet.[85]

Kelley recognizes that in the face of mystery, a person's concept of God does not necessarily help them make sense of events, which can exacerbate their suffering. In Robert's case for example, his concept of God did not help to ease his pain, but instead, made it more difficult to find meaning in the event.[86] Kelley's assessment of Robert's dilemma in finding meaning is accurate, but her conclusion seems vague and lacking any useful substance. From her Christian perspective, she offers this as a solution:

> "There is meaning in mystery. The Christian story is steeped in the Paschal mystery of Christ's suffering, death, and resurrection. And the heart of this mystery is love: God's fierce and faithful love for each person, manifest for all time in the life, death, and resurrection of Jesus Christ. 'For God so loved the world that he gave his only Son, so that everyone who believes in him may not perish but may have eternal life.' While life can seem scary and senseless in times of loss, its deepest meaning issues from a faithful God whose ways we can't fully know, but who is love. We cannot make human sense of every loss, but God is love."

How can this possibly be helpful? What does it even *mean*?

This would only add to Robert's confusion while discouraging theological exploration. In response to the question, "If God is love, then why would he cause me so much pain?" the answer given by Kelley seems to be, "Just believe in the doctrine." All this does is bring us right back to square one, in an endless dance of pointless circular reasoning. It is likely that Robert, David, Angie and the others whose stories are told here heard the exact same words from their pastors and church families. But the words didn't help. The promise of God's "fierce and faithful love" has little value for someone who feels abandoned or unfairly punished.

Petitionary and Intercessory prayer

The idea that God grants wishes can be just as disruptive to the grief healing process as the idea that God punishes us. How do we address the struggles of people like Corinne and David from the examples above, who relied so heavily on prayer?

In 2014 I attended a lecture by a man who had written a book about his experience with loss and grief. His infant daughter had died suddenly in 1990, and nine years later his wife died from a heart condition. Six years after that his 13 year-old son died of brain cancer. He described his spiritual response as follows:

> "Like most Americans, I was raised with a traditional Christian understanding of God, but I could not accept that a loving God would do this to me, so I sought the help of other gods. When my son was diagnosed, I asked every god I'd ever heard of to help me. I went to Catholic mass. I meditated with Buddhists. I participated in Native American ceremonies. I took my son to Chinese medicine practitioners and Shamanic healers. I uttered positive affirmations and visualized my son whole and healthy, calling on the laws of attraction along with the healing blood of Jesus. I prayed. I fasted. I cleaned my chakras and confessed my sins. But the kid died anyway."[87]

This man's experience may be the ultimate example of religious pluralism, and while it did not produce miracles, it *did* show him alternative ways to find meaning in his losses. His quest not only led to expanded spiritual awareness, it also launched his career as an author and lecturer with a large following of bereaved parents.

His prayers -- and the prayers of the other bereaved individuals mentioned here -- are a form of "petitionary prayer," in which the petitioner makes a specific request of entities such as gods, angels, or human beings who have special status, such as saints. Petitionary prayer may help the person doing the praying feel like they're taking action, but does it make a difference to God? In other words, can it influence the outcome of events?

It is generally believed that a prayer is considered "answered" if it produces the desired result, assuming that without the prayer, the outcome would have been different.[88] The same formula applies to "intercessory prayer," in which someone prays on behalf of someone else, for example, when a community prays to help a neighbor, or a hospital chaplain prays for a patient.

From my personal experience with petitionary prayer, I will share a story that I refer to as "the tree lesson." One weekend during my first year as a seminary student, my little house in the northern California redwoods was being battered by a fierce storm. The winds were so strong that the tall trees surrounding the house were swaying and bending, and the day before, the top half of a 30-foot cedar had fallen across my neighbor's driveway. I remember looking out my kitchen window at the trees blowing in the wind, and saying out loud, "Please don't let a tree fall on my house."

Who was I talking to? I immediately recognized that I was asking an imaginary third party to intervene, and I had to stop and ponder what it actually means to make such a request. I realized that my "prayer" was really just a way to express my fear. My heart was simply saying, "I'm vulnerable and afraid."

I recognized at that moment that giving our fears a voice produces a mild sense of comfort and relief, and also triggers a sense of personal responsibility that can empower us to seek concrete solutions to the problem. Conversely, directing the prayer outward -- to something "out there"-- can be a way of pushing the fear away so we don't have to face it or feel it.

In another personal example, I once witnessed a very strong act of intercessory prayer at a community food bank, where before the food was handed out to the needy, one of the organizers led a group prayer. She called upon Jesus to help all the people in the room, and specifically, to heal Mr. Brown's arthritis, help Mrs. Green find the money to get her roof fixed, to make sure Mrs. Jones has a healthy baby, and to bless Timmy Thompson on the occasion of his high school graduation.

Perhaps it was her meek, pleading tone of voice, or perhaps it was her assumption that impassioned entreaties can make things turn out the way we want them to, but I found her prayer to be very disempowering. It presented an image of humanity as confused, helpless sheep who are lost without a shepherd to take care of them. While the analogy of sheep and shepherd is a common Christian theme, Pastor Greg Laurie recognizes that being compared to a sheep is not a compliment, because, as he bluntly states it, sheep are "the dumbest of all creatures." They have no survival skills and cannot fend for themselves, so they are completely dependent on the shepherd.[89] While the people at the food bank certainly depended on the food distributed there, a prayer that confirms their sense of powerlessness does little to lift them up. If it were up to me, I would have offered a prayer of gratitude for being part of a supportive community, and a meditation to connect them to their hearts, their innate divine nature, and their ability to tap in to inner strength.

Episcopal Bishop John Shelby Spong says "The intervening God who answers our intercessory prayers is a comfortable fiction that is no longer worthy of our worship... The Santa Claus view of God keeps us in a childlike state, but if we can allow ourselves to grow up, we can own the beauty and power of our humanity as we explore new definitions of faith for the 21st century."[90]

A God That Punishes Us

I said earlier that mythical stories have immense value for unifying communities and establishing a shared set of beliefs and moral codes. When myth can be separated from meaning, and stories understood as metaphors and allegories, a culture can gain wisdom and spiritual guidance from the messages within the stories. But that value can easily be missed when the stories are interpreted as literal, historical events, and our view of what could be a vast spiritual panorama becomes narrow and one-dimensional. When taken literally, the depiction of God in the Hebrew Bible presents a father figure who is easily angered and demands absolute, unwavering obedience. The slightest infraction can result in catastrophic punishment, not only for the perpetrator, but for thousands of innocents who happen to be standing in the line of fire.

Most of us who were raised in Judeo-Christian theology were introduced to this god as children, and some of us grew up feeling that we were flawed, unworthy, shameful and even despised by God. Language that could be considered nothing short of terrorizing became firmly seated in Christian culture based in part on the words of Jonathan Edwards in *Sinners in the Hands of an Angry God.* Edwards made the case that the "wicked" ancient Israelites deserved God's wrath and were justifiably punished for not observing the laws faithfully enough. He warned his congregation that we are all vulnerable to this sort of punishment, because "There is nothing that keeps wicked men at any one moment out of hell, but the mere pleasure of God."[91]

For bereaved persons who think their losses are punishment for some sort of wrongdoing in their lives, the good news is that not all Christian ministries believe in divine punishment... at least not for their own flocks. Many of today's contemporary Christian teachings denounce the belief in a punishing God,[92] and one Jehovah's Witness website even poses the very astute question, "Why would Jesus heal sick people if God was punishing them?"[93]

But these messages are confusing, because if we scratch the surface of some of these statements, we find that according to some interpretations, the reprieve from punishment only applies to followers of Jesus. A headline on the *GraceLife International* website proclaims that the idea of God punishing people is a myth. But further down the page, the author, Mark Maulding, states emphatically, "God does not punish us who are in Christ! He cannot! Because all of His anger for our sins was placed on Jesus on His cross." Maulding further explains, "We were tried for our crimes of sin and found guilty. Our sentence was death, but Jesus took our place and died for us. As a result, we cannot be found guilty again by God."[94]

What is a bereaved person to make of this, especially if the person does not identify as being one of "us who are in Christ?" Does this mean that only the followers of Jesus are spared from God's wrath, but everybody else deserves it? Even if the griever *is* a devoted Christian, (as in Kelley's examples), why would they still feel they are being punished, despite the doctrinal assurance that they are immune to punishment?

Heaven vs. Hell

I have supported -- and grieved with -- many people whose loved ones have died by suicide. For many Christians, in addition to the burden of grief and guilt, the griever is plagued by theological questions about whether suicides go to hell. One Christian website offers this range of possible answers:[95]

- All Christians who commit suicide will go straight to hell.

- All Christians who commit suicide will go straight to heaven because they cannot lose their salvation with the Lord.

- God will judge each case individually.

The author concludes that #3 is the most likely scenario, since every case is different, and God might be more lenient with the mentally ill or someone who has been influenced by demons. The other two options are saddled by the burdensome question of whether Christians can lose their salvation. The author believes that yes, salvation can be lost when a Christian enters a dark side activity guided by demons with no intention of letting the Lord help him/her out of it. Since suicide is similar to murder, the author believes, it is one of the worse sins you can possibly commit against the Lord, but with the "correct spiritual warfare strategy," the demons can be vanquished.[96]

During my hospital chaplaincy rounds, I once encountered a patient who said something startling. He was in his early 70s, and had just been diagnosed with a life-threatening disease for which there was no intervention. He'd been reflecting on death and the afterlife, and requested a chaplain visit. When I arrived, he told me that he was concerned about going to hell because he'd lived a sinful life. This is how he posed the question:

Patient: Where do you think Muslims go in the afterlife?

Chaplain: I don't know. I can't say for certain where anybody goes when they die. What's more important right now is what *you* think about the afterlife.

Patient: I think they go to hell because they worship Buddha. They believe in false gods. They can't possibly go to the same heaven that Christians go to.

My immediate response was to feel repulsed by this man's ignorance, and my instinct was to correct him ("Actually sir, Muslims don't worship Buddha"). But my job was not to educate him in comparative religion or to judge him. I was there to help him with his quandary as compassionately as possible. I knew that he was really asking about where *he* might go in the afterlife. Based on his beliefs, good people go to heaven and bad people go to hell, and he was afraid he might have to spend eternity among the bad people, which, in his reasoning, include Muslims and Buddhists.

He described himself as a "believer in Christ," a "strong Christian" and a "repentant sinner." My response to this was to point out that as a follower of Jesus, according to his faith, he is saved and forgiven. Redemption is guaranteed, so if he is faithful, he can be at peace knowing that he will be welcomed into the eternal life that his faith promises. But even though this might have provided some comfort, his doubts persisted, because his actual, lived experience told him something different. He had not personally *experienced* any direct revelation that made his belief in redemption seem real. He did not *feel* forgiven, and he wanted some sort of sign or assurance of his salvation.

And here's where the circular reasoning comes in… according to his beliefs, if he is seeking reassurance, it means that his faith isn't strong enough. And if his faith isn't strong enough, then he is not truly saved, in which case he might indeed end up in the same afterlife as the non-believers. It was, understandably, a monumental conflict for him. Running on this hamster wheel was causing him extreme distress at a time when he could have been focused on acceptance, forgiveness and meaning-making.

This man never told me what his exact sins were, but our conversation prompted the question, what specific behaviors constitute an eternity of punishment in the afterlife? Catholicism teaches that a sin must meet three criteria in order to be "mortal" or "deadly" (deserving of eternal damnation if not confessed, or if the sinner does not make a "perfect act of contrition" before death). These conditions are:[97]

- The sin must be a "grave matter," which means that the act itself is intrinsically evil and immoral, such as murder, rape, incest, etc.

- The person must have full knowledge that what they are doing is evil and immoral.

- The person must freely choose to commit the act.

This is a specifically Catholic doctrine, but other Christian denominations also have long lists of sinful behaviors that carry the threat of divine punishment. One Christian website has a list of "40 Sins That Will Send You to Hell," and it includes, in addition to the grave matters of murder and rape, a list of lesser crimes that include profanity, rebellion against parents, evil thoughts, sexual intercourse before marriage, homosexuality, blasphemy and entering marriage under the false pretense of being a virgin.[98]

Although the Catholic church has relaxed some of its restrictions in recent decades, there are many in today's world who still embrace the older traditions. A Nigerian Catholic blogsite offers a long list of mortal sins that includes divorce, contraception, extreme anger, masturbation, encouragement of another's sins, suicide, pornography, and failing to attend mass.[99] My friend Fr. Coman Dalton (another former priest) says that even though divorce, contraception, missing mass and even suicide are no longer widely considered by the church to be mortal sins, many people, especially older people, still cling to these old ideas. And these ideas are not uniquely Catholic. They have blended into Christian thinking over time and across denominations.[100]

For grievers, the old ideas, and many of the new ones, can complicate the mourning process by adding fear, superstition and guilt into an already burdensome set of tasks. Bishop Spong observes that the old system of reward and punishment to control behavior must be discarded if we are to enter a more mature relationship with Christianity.[101]

And that maturing is well underway. According to research by religion professor and Christian theologian Elizabeth Drescher, the idea of hell is becoming less of a threat for American believers, and the idea of heaven is also losing some of its appeal. Over the last two decades, she reports, adherence to institutional religion and belief in God has declined, and with it, the belief in heaven and hell.[102]

Belief in Satan

Progressive theologian Kevin Forrester explains that biblical sources characterized "the satan" as the presence of an oppositional force, or anything we encounter that is in an adversarial position. The concept became anthropomorphized in later teachings so that God could have an opponent onto which we could project our internal struggles while also blaming it for anything that harms or challenges us. Forrester points out that the Greek term "diabolos," which was translated later as "devil," literally means "one who throws something across one's path."[103]

In a perspective that sees human experience as divided into dueling forces of good (God) and evil (Satan), many assume that everything good comes from God and everything bad comes from Satan. In this view, loss, trauma, abandonment, depression, sadness, violence, anger and even death can be avoided, and if they do occur, it is either a punishment or a great cosmic error, as frequently expressed by many grievers who lost their loved ones "before their time." [104]

Granted this might be an extreme view, but it is promoted by evangelical ministers like Patrick Kelly, who preaches:

> "Suffering is an instrument of Satan... It is Satan who wants to see the drug addict use, the alcoholic drink, the weak fall down, and the ego-filled self-implode... it is not God's will that anyone should suffer... We must understand that suffering eats away at faith. Trauma undermines faith. It is Satan's goal, by whatever means necessary, to see that you turn as far away from Christ as possible. Suffering and pain are Satan's weapons against you." [105]

On my hospital chaplaincy rounds I once encountered a patient who was so steeped in her fear of Satan that it severely compromised her health. She was morbidly obese and had multiple medical issues. She was hospitalized because she'd suddenly decided to stop taking all her medications, and within two days she was in the emergency room. She attributed her irrational behavior and what she called her "overly emotional state of mind" to Satan, because he is responsible for strong emotions, which are sinful. She also said, "We can't trust the bad things in life or the good things. Because even the good things come from Satan tricking us."

Mystic theologian Deepak Chopra outlines the differences between cultures that believe in Satan as opposed to cultures that do not:

Chopra's Analysis of the Concept of Satan[106]

SATAN IS REAL WHEN...	SATAN IS UNREAL WHEN...
A culture believes in the Satan myth	A culture is aware of how myths are made
Believers pay attention to that myth and give it value	People are self-aware and take responsibility for their own emotions
Guilt is projected outward onto demons instead of healed inside	There is a belief in forgiveness, healing and atonement
Wrongdoing accumulates without a means for finding forgiveness, atonement or purification	Outlets for negative energies are found through therapy, open dialog, healthy family dynamics, education, etc.
Children are put in fear of demons and told that demons have supernatural powers.	Children are not conditioned to believe in demons and other supernatural enemies

A more self-empowered culture takes ownership of its behavior, and as such, might interpret heaven and hell as something for which we are personally responsible and capable of controlling. Hell would be seen as a lower level of consciousness characterized by a sense of separation and disconnection from divine source/God, while heaven would be seen as a level of higher consciousness in which we see ourselves as part of God rather than separate from it. Both of these possibilities exist within us rather than in a remote location.[107] Instead of being operated and monitored by a third-party entity that exists in a separate sphere, we are, instead, empowered by an internal engine that directs us toward moral behavior, so there is nothing to be saved from or to be judged for. In this scenario, judging and salvation are a matter of personal responsibility rather than divine micromanagement.

Some conservative Christians disagree resolutely with this, and find toxicity in progressive theologies specifically because those theologies do *not* include Satan, divine punishment, biblical literalism and salvation through Jesus. For example, *Today's Christian Woman* magazine warns readers to be wary of ideas that come from sources other than the Bible, and to mistrust teachings that suggest one can reach a higher level of spirituality through works (vs. faith).[108] A Christian website called *The Spiritual Research Network* publishes a long list of "dangerous spiritual practices" that include yoga, Kabbalah, centering prayer and reading Carl Jung.[109] And *Charisma News* claims that "any form of meditation, apart from biblical meditation, is opening the door wide to the enemy... Any time we mix Christian discipline with any other religious practice, we anger God."[110] Similarly, evangelical lay minister Andy Roman laments the findings of a recent Gallup Poll showing that only one in four Americans believe the Bible is the actual word of God and is to be taken literally. He feels that rejecting literalism is a dangerous movement that "emboldens anarchy."[111]

Bargaining with God

Although Dr. Elizabeth Kubler Ross was not a theologian, and her widely misunderstood stage theory about coping with grief was intended for terminally ill patients facing their own imminent deaths rather than for those grieving the deaths of others, her observations about the bargaining stage are relevant here.[112] A person coping with acute grief wants nothing more than to stop their pain, even if it involves unrealistic fantasies of bringing a departed loved one back to life, or turning the clock back as if the event never happened. In acute grief, we desperately want to return to our lives as they were before the loss occurred, and our thoughts are filled with strategies for making this happen. But while a few mythical biblical heroes were able to bargain with God,[113] it doesn't generally work that way for the rest of us.

One of my seminary classmates -- I'll call her Dorothy -- shares an amusing family story about the circumstances surrounding her conception. In 1948, a year before Dorothy was born, her older brother was in the hospital in critical condition and close to death. Dorothy's mother, Angela, stood vigil at her son's bedside. Angela was a devout Catholic, and believed that the reason her son was dying was because God was punishing her for using contraception. She would have done anything to save her son, so she made a deal with God, promising to stop using contraception if God would let her son recover.

Her son did recover, and a year later Angela gave birth to her second child, my classmate Dorothy. Angela honored her side of the bargain and had stopped using birth control, and she believed that in exchange for her promise, God had honored his. But did God actually participate in this deal? Was there a negotiation in which two parties agreed upon a set of terms?

In Chapter 4 we will meet Steve, who'd asked God for only one thing in his life... to keep his children safe. After Steve's daughter and son were both killed in a car crash, he became obsessed with anger at God for not honoring the agreement. But there wasn't technically an *agreement*. There was only Steve's wish that his children would be safe... a wish that every parent has.

In the next chapter we will be introduced to God on Trial, a stage play in which a group of Jewish prisoners in a World War II concentration camp put God on trial for breaking the promise of special blessings for the Jewish people. In the mock trial, the men quoted scripture as evidence of God's promise. But unless one is interpreting biblical stories literally, we have no reason the think that God can make deals with humanity in general, much less with individual humans seeking relief from their suffering.

3

When Bad Things Happen to Good People

To begin an investigation of toxic theology, we must first consider, as a foundation, the theological view that characterizes God as a humanoid figure with two opposing faces. One is the face of a loving parent/trusted protector, and the other is the face of a harsh parent/ unreliable protector. With this opposition informing our deepest theological uncertainties, where can traumatized people place their faith? Can we learn to be comfortable with the tension between the two faces? Can anger be directed at the harsh parent/unreliable protector while still having faith that the loving parent/reliable protector is present? Viewed from another perspective, if God only has one face, and that face is supposed to be goodness and love, then how do we explain suffering?

The question of why a loving God would allow tragedy to befall even the most pious person is ancient and universal, and has plagued humanity since the onset of monotheistic thought. For many religious people, suffering is seen as either a punishment for sin, interference by Satan, or a random experience that belongs to the realm of mystery, beyond our ability to understand. As evangelical

Christian scholars Maxwell and Perrine described in their analysis of *The Problem of God in the Presence of Grief*:

> "For some, God's presence brings various forms of positive aid to the process of grief... Yet, for others, God's presence further compounds difficulty and guilt. For some, sadness over loss is well understood, whereas in others it is perceived as a lack of sufficient faith in God... The danger of addressing grief with theology is that it can inevitably reduce a complex and often bewildering phenomenon to a constraining ideology that may even result in the imposition of harm rather than relief. The helpfulness of God for grief is therefore not uniformly felt."[114]

I do not presume to know why bad things happen to good people. But I *do* know that there are ways to incorporate spirituality into grief work that do not rely on traditional definitions of good vs. bad experiences or conventional qualifiers of faith. I also know that for those who have not ventured beyond scriptural literalism and traditional doctrines, these questions repeatedly surface in the wake of trauma:

1. Is suffering randomly dispensed by an all-powerful God for reasons beyond our understanding?

2. Is suffering a punishment for bad (unfaithful, non-believing) behavior?

3. Does devotion and faithfulness guarantee safety and protection?

4. If the god of the Hebrew Bible promised his chosen people abundant rewards in exchange for devotion and obedience, then how do we explain the holocaust?

5. If Jesus died for our sins and the stain of original sin was cleansed from humanity, then why was sin not removed from the world with his death?

Bishop Spong asks us to consider whether God can still be real if we dismiss all images of God as a parent and personalistic deity. He proposes that this question can be answered by simply shifting the way we look at human experience, and that we can begin by referring to God as a "what" instead of a "who."[115] Imagine referring to God as "it" instead of "he" (or "she"). Imagine how different our relationship with the spiritual realm would be if we used language such as "*It* created us," or "*It* is all-powerful."

I once suggested this to a woman I met at a conference, and she was horrified. She said, "God's going to punish you for calling him an *it*."

Human beings create religious doctrines and dogmas to explain existence, rationalize suffering and control behavior. Noted philosopher and psychologist William James said that we create gods that are useful to us because they reinforce the demands we make on ourselves and on others.[116] In other words, our images of God are *projections*. Bishop Spong postulates that the Western mystics perceived the idea of a personal god as only a transitory stage in human development (similar to the what Fowler described in the stages of faith development). Spong cautions us to remember that the spiritual quest is an interior journey rather than an exterior one.[117]

The ancient Israelites assigned religious meaning to their misfortunes by deciding that God was punishing them for their sins,[118] which assumes there is also a converse action whereby God rewards *good* deeds. But as we learn from the stories of every righteous person that has ever suffered, the reward/punishment model does not stand up to scrutiny.

Shattered Assumptions

We go through our lives holding on to certain assumptions about how the world works. If we didn't believe, for example, that marriages should last forever and children shouldn't die before their parents, we would be less likely to risk getting married or having children. Psychology professor Ronni Janoff-Bulman suggests that there are three fundamental assumptions common in Western thinking: [119]

- The world is benevolent
- The world is meaningful
- The self is worthy

We can find examples of this in our society's list of moral "shoulds," including:

- Bad things shouldn't happen to good people
- If I'm faithful in my religion, I should be protected by God
- A child should not die before its parents
- If I treat others well, they should treat me well in return

There are also mundane, day-to-day assumptions that are critical to our functioning. We assume that:

- When we drive to work or fly on a plane, we will arrive safely.
- Our job will support us so we can buy a house and get a dog.
- We will keep that house until we decide to sell it.
- The dog won't get hit by a car or bite the mailman.
- Our spouse is faithful
- Our children are safe at school

We cannot survive without these assumptions. If we didn't cling to them, we would never buy a house, get a dog, drive a car or send our children to school. We would not take any risks at all. Life would *stop*.

Janoff-Bulman tells us that our theories about how life works are organized in a hierarchy, with our most basic assumptions being the most generalized and abstract. These assumptions are based on an expectation of safety in the world. They compose "the bedrock of our conceptual system," so they are the assumptions we are least likely challenge.[120] When tragic events challenge these expectations, a state of mind is created that Janoff-Bulman calls "conceptual disintegration." In this state, she tells us, "previous notions about the value of the self have been brutally broken, leaving the traumatized person feeling small, powerless and weak in a world without kindness or beneficence... the opposite of the world one occupied before the event."[121]

This shock to the system -- this dark night of the soul -- can apply to the way we respond to losses of any kind, whether a death, a divorce, loss of a job, loss of health, loss of a role or identity, or any circumstance that forces us to re-evaluate our understanding of the three primary assumptions. The natural death of an 85 year-old man is predictable and expected, and although his loved ones will grieve, such a death does not challenge our assumptions about how life is supposed to work. However, a tragic, unexpected loss -- a betrayal of trust, the death of a young person, natural disasters, or any death by violence -- will cause us to question our assumption that the world is safe, meaningful and benevolent.

Biblical scholar Walter Brueggemann, in discussing his book *Reality, Grief and Hope*, looks at how cultural groups and nations can be shaken out of their sense of exceptionalism when a traumatic communal loss occurs. He specifically cites the exile of the Israelites in the sixth century BCE and the 9/11 terrorist attacks in the United States. In both cases, the victimized group had a sense of entitlement, either as a special protection from God or as an impenetrable political power in the world. When that protection failed, the group was shocked into a new awareness of its vulnerability.[122]

A disruption in beliefs about safety and justice will prompt either the acceptance of a new world based on what Janoff-Bulman calls "powerful new data,"[123] or clinging to an old reality that is no longer viable. This is a pivotal choice in the healing process, and if a grieving or traumatized person cannot shift into a new understanding of reality and the new world that accompanies it, he/she is at risk for *complicated grief* (which will be discussed in Chapter Four).

The Book of Job

The ancient Israelites attempted to directly address the question of suffering in *The Book of Job*, which explored these themes in terms of human suffering:

- Is loyalty to God rewarded?
- Does God punish us?
- Does God test us?
- The importance of questioning God
- The apparent randomness of suffering

Janoff-Bulman says the popularity of the Book of Job is a reflection of our attachment to the three basic human assumptions of benevolence, meaningfulness and worthiness.[124] This is why we are so uncomfortable with the juxtaposition between Job's suffering and his innocence.[125]

Bishop Spong refers to the Book of Job as "an icon of new consciousness"[126] because it forces us to look at the absence of fairness in human experience. He reminds us that one of the pillars of Jewish thought is the idea that one who obeys the laws and worships God properly will be rewarded, and if one does not do this, the vengeance of God is sure to follow. This idea establishes a system of organization, logic and purpose vs. chaos and meaninglessness.[127] But Job's situation -- as a righteous man who lost everything for no apparent reason -- turned that logic upside down. If blessings can't be earned and wrongdoing isn't punished, then where is the logic, safety and predictability in life?

Richard Elliott Friedman, an author, scholar and professor of Jewish studies, offers this explanation of how the reward and punishment system originated in Jewish theology. As he explains it, during the Israelites' exile in Babylon in 500 BCE, because their history and culture was threatened with extinction, they began to *write* their story, which for the past 1000 years had only been transmitted orally. They needed to create a strong presence that could stand up to the oppressive regimes that surrounded them, so they constructed the image of a powerful god that promised special benefits to their tribe, including victory over their enemies.

The way the scribes packaged these concepts was based on the assumption that God is "fair," and as such, good people would be rewarded while bad people would be punished.[128] But if the writing of the Pentateuch (the first five books of the bible, which are also the *Torah*; the cornerstone of Jewish law and history), did occur during this period of exile, it would have been difficult for the oppressed people to trust in these promises, since finding themselves without a homeland would imply that either God's promises had been broken, or the tribe had committed some grievous error for which they were now being punished. Special protection by God was nowhere to be found at this point in Jewish history, so the writing that took place reflected the tribe's grief and sense of powerlessness. To justify their loss of status and security, it was necessary to invent an unpredictable, punitive god who was angry at them for a variety of transgressions. As Friedman states, "In Pagan religion, if another nation defeats you, you can say their god was more powerful than your god. But in monotheism, if you're suffering, it must be because you did something wrong"[129]

The Book of Job attempts to show that punishment isn't the only explanation. Although it offers no real conclusion or concrete guidance, it does give us permission to question, which is perhaps its most valuable gift. If we view the world in terms of justice (in this context, a "just god"), then the world tends be divided into the consequences of good vs. bad behavior, in which positive events are rewards and negative events are punishment.[130] But that leaves the bereaved, the oppressed, the marginalized, the sick, the homeless, the lonely and everyone else who is suffering to think that punishment is the reason for their misfortune. Morrow tells us that "the over-controlling monotheism of perfectionist retribution theology is shown to deprive suffering persons of dignity and hope for life." He sees the theology of Job as a repressive and toxic belief system that betrays the dignity of God, the cosmos and humanity.[131]

In Job's world, the popular thinking of the day was based on the idea that humanity is at the center of the universe and the pinnacle of creation. Job's experience asks him to consider a complete theological renovation; a reconstruction of his view of the universe and the structure of his world. Traumatic events, loss and grief invite us to do the same… to re-vision and rebuild our definition of how the world and the universe works. As Morrow says, removing the anthropomorphic view of God, and understanding that the cosmos does not have humanity at its center can be therapeutic and healing, relieving suffering by sparing us from seeing every bad experience as something for which we can be blamed.[132]

God on Trial

In 2008, a British screenwriter created a television play called *God on Trial*,[133] which was based on a story from Elie Wiesel's 1995 book *The Trial of God*. The play is set in the Auschwitz concentration camp in World War II, and the characters are a group of Jewish prisoners, among them, a rabbi, a physicist, and a law professor. The group struggles with the conflict between their religious beliefs and the horrific world in which they now find themselves. In an attempt to make sense of why the god who promised them security and protection would now allow them to experience unimaginable suffering with little hope for rescue, the men enact a mock trial for the person they believe is responsible for their dilemma... God. They accuse God of "breach of contract" for breaking his covenant with the Jewish people. After all, they reasoned, if the Torah is the law, then the law has been broken.

In the mock trial, each man played a role, such as a prosecutor, defense attorney and expert witnesses. All of Jewish history and theology was questioned on the witness stand, including the exodus story, the covenant with Abraham and the violent acts committed by Yahweh throughout the Hebrew Bible. The primary question in their case was whether or not God is "good." Inquiries from the prosecution included:

- During the plagues of Egypt, why did God let Pharaoh live, but killed all the children? How could this possibly convince the mothers of Egypt that the God of the Israelites was just? [134]

- Why did God wait until the soldiers were crossing through the opening in the Red Sea to close the waters back up, drowning them all? Why didn't he just close the waters after the Israelites had safely crossed, sparing the lives of the soldiers? [135]

- Why did God command his people to destroy the communities that were already established in the promised land, rather than allowing the Israelites to live peacefully among them? [136]

- God rejected Saul as King because he didn't obey God's command to kill all the people and animals in Amalek. Saul killed men, women and children, as instructed, but spared the Kenites and the best sheep and cattle (to feed his army). God rejected him as king because he didn't obey to the letter.[137]

- David killed Bathsheba's husband Uriah against the wishes of God. Did God strike David or Bathsheba? No. He punished their child with a torturous death.[138]

Their verdict provoked a sweeping range of contrasting interpretations, justifications and further questioning that challenged the magical thinking of their theology:[139]

- God is just, so we must have done something wrong.
- God is our enemy. He has made a new covenant with someone else.
- How would it be if this is not a punishment, but a purification? What if those who survive this would live in an age of wisdom, understanding and knowledge? What if some great good were to come of this?"
- It's all written down. It's a covenant. God is in breach of contract.

- Did God not also make the Egyptians, and the Amaleks, and the Moabites? God is smiting us now, the same way he smote them. They fell, as we are falling. And what did they learn? They learned that our god is not good. He was never good.
They learned the he was only on *our* side.

One of the most thought-provoking comments -- which prompts us to think rationally instead of magically -- came from the physicist, who said, "God made a hundred thousand million stars, and each one might have a planetary system like ours revolving around it. So why would this god focus his attention on humans, and on Jews in particular? It is simply wrong. An illusion. We are not at the center of the universe."[140]

Frank Rogers, professor of spiritual formation at Claremont School of Theology, tells us that compassion is considered a cornerstone teaching of the Jewish Torah.[141] But Yahweh's behavior throughout the Hebrew Bible is anything but compassionate. So with contradiction built in to the fabric of our religious education, it is understandable that a traumatized person cannot connect the dots when a supposedly compassionate God inflicts unimaginable pain on its creations.

Since the beginning of the 19th century, most scholars have come to support a theory called the *documentary hypothesis,* which addresses the ways in which the Bible's first books were written and assembled. The hypothesis states that writers in antiquity created numerous written works over hundreds of years, and that these documents were used as sources for later writers and editors who "wrote" the Bible as we know it. To date, as Friedman explains, scholars have identified four different schools of authorship for the Pentateuch, and have dated the writing of these books to the period of the Jewish exile in Babylon in the sixth century BCE.[142]

Yet millions of the faithful believe that these books were written by Moses during the Israelites' exodus from Egypt, even though there is no archeological evidence that such a mass exodus even occurred, or that the Israelites were ever enslaved by Egypt at all.[143] The cultural attachment to a literal belief that God promised the land of Canaan to his chosen people is at the core of the conflict between Israel and Palestine today. Yet very few people who have passionate opinions about this conflict are aware that it is based on the myth that there is a god who likes some people better than others, makes promises, and negotiates real estate deals.

If, as archeological evidence and historical inquiry suggests, most of the Hebrew Bible was written during the Jewish exile in Babylon, it leaves a large gap between the written record and the events of 1000 years earlier that the record is describing. The land that we now know as Israel was not a powerful kingdom, but a small town or village overshadowed by the enormous power of Babylon and Egypt. Friedman suggests that its leaders and priests, in order to establish a sense of power that could compete with other nations, created the idea of an all-powerful god that took a special liking to their tribe and promised to transform them into a great nation.[144] This idea, mixed with stories and legends handed down verbally for centuries, found its way into the writings of the scribes who wrote while in exile. They had heard for generations, through oral tradition, that they had been promised God's favor and would become world leaders if they followed God's laws. But now they found themselves imprisoned in a foreign land with no nation, no temple for worship, no identity, no political or social power and no special protection from God. In writing their story, they had to find a way to justify their loss of status in God's eyes.

Literal interpretation of stories like these, where God makes special deals with special people and then punishes them brutally for not following the letter of the law, creates a foundation for judgment and separation rather than peace and harmony; self-loathing rather than personal empowerment; and a relationship with the divine that is based on fear rather than love.

Allegory vs. Actuality

Dr. Steven Hairfield compiled an amazing analysis of biblical symbolism in his book, *A Metaphysical Interpretation of the Bible*. He focused a lot of his attention on the exodus story, encouraging the reader to see it as an allegory that expresses the journey from material enslavement to spiritual awareness. Similarly, psychiatrist Robert Rosenthal, who specializes in the interplay between psychotherapy and spirituality, suggests that we interpret the conflict between Moses and Pharaoh as representing the tension between the material and the spiritual world; Pharaoh is hopelessly earthbound, clinging to wealth, power and dominance, while Moses represents the higher ideal of breaking the bonds of attachment to the material world.[145]

Hairfield and Rosenthal both inspired me to look more deeply into metaphysical interpretations of the Exodus story, and when I discovered that the writings of third century Christian theologian Origen of Alexandria also looked at it through a symbolic lens, I was enchanted. Origen described the enslaved people as being "afflicted by mortar and brick,"[146] which symbolizes the heavy density and limitations of our physical bodies. But by the end of the journey, the people end up "watered by the waves of divine knowledge,"[147] which is an expression of lightness and transcendence. The spiritual quest begins when we realize that we are enslaved by identifying exclusively with the material world, and throughout our lives, we seek freedom from that state as we move toward mystical union.

Origen also speaks of a "double Exodus"[148] through which we leave not only our enslaved status behind, but our uninitiated selves as well. The uninitiated self is removed from the soul's divine nature; a state of existence that Origen refers to as being "gentile," or *an outsider*. Once we begin the journey back to divine unity, we are no longer strangers, and are welcomed back home. In the exodus story, the people spent 40 years wandering in the desert. Forty years would have been a typical lifespan at that time, and spending those years as bereft wanderers represents a lifetime of hunger and spiritual seeking, beginning with spiritual starvation, homelessness and deprivation, and traveling toward a spiritual home where sustenance awaits.

The point of this analysis is to illustrate that the story is an *allegory*, not a factual entry in the historical record. Origen teaches us to use our critical thinking and intuitive interpretation skills when reading spiritual texts. The sense of exile and desire for reunion is not a story belonging to one group of people or one point in time. It is the eternal story of humanity's struggle to reconcile flesh and spirit.

If we take these stories literally, we deprive ourselves of the healing intention with which they were created. Strip away the literalism, and much of the toxicity will disappear with it.

4

Bereavement and Bad Theology: A Toxic Cocktail

Before we begin discussing grief that has been complicated by toxic theology, let's first look at the various types of losses that can trigger a grief response. The categories below come from Mitchell & Anderson's book, *All our Losses, All our Griefs,* [149] which is widely used for training chaplains, ministers and other spiritual care providers. The examples and explanations are my own:

Types of Losses

Material -- Loss of a home, friends and community if you move to another city; loss of an object or material wealth (car breaking down, bankruptcy, stock market crash); loss of familiar surroundings (house fire, foreclosure, changing a child's bedroom after she leaves home, or after the death of a child). These are losses that can be seen clearly in the physical world. They are material, visual, tangible and touchable.

Relationship -- A loss due to death, divorce or estrangement is the *direct* loss of a relationship. But this can be also be experienced *indirectly*, for example, when friends and/or family pull away after your divorce (because they've chosen sides), or after the death of your loved one (because death and grief makes them uncomfortable).

Functional -- This refers to the loss of physical or mental health and functionality. There is a grieving process that accompanies a diagnosis, another that accompanies living with the loss of mental or physical function, and yet another for anticipating death if the diagnosis is life-threatening.

System Loss -- When the systems we rely on to support and protect us can no longer be trusted, we grieve the loss of that system. These systems can include governments, corporations, social groups, families and religions.

Intrapsychic and Role Loss -- The loss of *self* can result from any of the losses mentioned above. When our beliefs and assumptions are shattered and our sense of place in the world comes into question, we are unsure of our role, our purpose and our identity. If your husband dies, you lose your role as a wife. If your only child dies, you lose your role as a parent. If you lose your job (or retire), you can no longer identify as employee or an executive. If you lose your house, you are no longer a homeowner.

Anticipated/Unanticipated -- The death of a loved one after a lengthy illness is an anticipated loss for which we can prepare. The same thing is true for the end of a marriage that has been disintegrating for years. By contrast, a sudden, unexpected death or abandonment is *unanticipated*, and adds shock and disbelief to the grief experience.

Actual vs. imagined -- Imagining a loss that hasn't actually happened is a key feature of post-traumatic stress syndrome. The traumatized person, having experienced a similar loss in the past, is never really at ease in present time, and lives in a state of heightened vigilance, expecting the loss to occur again.

Building upon the types of losses that Mitchel and Anderson have identified, I offer the following additions:

Sympathetic Loss -- Identifying with -- and feeling the pain of -- other people's losses.

Collective Loss -- Shared pain and grief in a community, for example, when a natural disaster or school shooting occurs.

Tribal/National Loss -- A displaced, oppressed or marginalized group experiences this type of loss, and the grief can be transferred from one generation to the next. For example, Native Americans, Hawaiians and Africans who lost their culture due to colonization and slavery.

Relinquishment Loss -- When we voluntarily choose to give something up, there is a grief that accompanies that relinquishment. This can apply to leaving a relationship, selling a house or giving up a habit such as smoking or drinking. Even though the relinquishment may be a positive one that will improve your life, the lost object or habit is missed and mourned.

As you read through the list above, you will notice that many of these losses intersect with one another, and they are shared with those around us. The grief response ripples through the social group, family and community, each experiencing it from their own unique perspective. A man who becomes disabled due to an illness or accident grieves for his functional loss, but also experiences role loss because he can no longer be the family breadwinner, and perhaps even system loss if he feels the medical establishment has failed him, or if his religious beliefs didn't provide the protection and comfort he expected. His family, friends and close associates also experience these losses, but from a different vantage point.

Grief does not unfold in a linear fashion, nor can it be experienced in isolation. It is a complex web of interactions that transform us from the ground up... starting at our earthly roots and reaching into the highest realms of spiritual awareness.

What is Complicated Grief?

The religious beliefs of a grieving person -- and the beliefs of others in that person's sphere of influence, such as friends, family and community -- can have a profound impact on the grief healing trajectory. If the religious beliefs are toxic, they can sometimes trigger a maladaptive response, which is known by several terms, including *complicated grief, complicated mourning* or *prolonged grief disorder.* Here are some definitions of complicated grief by two of today's leading researchers in the field:

Therese Rando:
"A generic term indicating that, given the amount of time since the death, there is some compromise, distortion or failure of one or more of the processes of mourning."[150]

William Worden:
"The intensification of grief to the level where the person is overwhelmed, resorts to maladaptive behavior, or remains interminably in the state of grief without progression of the mourning process to completion."[151]

Worden recognizes four specific tasks in the process of "normal" grieving:[152]

1. Accepting the reality of the loss
2. Work through the pain of grief
3. Adjust to an environment in which the deceased is missing
4. Emotionally relocate the deceased and move on with life

When these tasks cannot be navigated successfully, grief can become complicated if the following responses are present:[153]

- **Prolonged Grief** -- The griever is aware that grief is not resolving after many months or years since the loss event.

- **Delayed Grief** -- The griever's emotions are thwarted, even though they might have had an emotional response at the time of the loss.

- **Exaggerated Grief** -- Characterized by excessive anxiety, depression or anger that may impair the person's normal functioning.

- **Somatic or Behavioral Symptoms** -- The griever is experiencing physical symptoms or behavioral problems without being aware that unresolved grief may be at the core of the issue.

Rando identifies six critical tasks that are necessary for a healthy trajectory of healing, and refers to them as the "Six Rs of Mourning"[154] In the following chart, I've used her Six Rs to show how toxic theology might express itself through each of those tasks, based on selected examples from cases I've encountered in my teaching, counseling and chaplaincy work (names and identifiable details have been changed):

RANDO'S SIX R'S OF MOURNING	BELIEFS THAT CAN COMPLICATE THE TASKS
1. Recognize the loss -- When the mourner is unwilling or unable to accept that the loss has occurred, this important primary task can be thwarted.	A rural African mother brought her dead baby to the village church and asked the priest to revive the child. She said, "Jesus could raise the dead, so why can't you?"
2. React to the separation -- Mourners who are unwilling or unable to fully experience the pain of the loss will have difficulty with this task.	The parents of a murdered child will not allow themselves to acknowledge their anger because they believe that anger is a sin.
3. Recollect and re-experience the deceased and the relationship -- If the circumstances of the death or the deceased's lifestyle is viewed as sinful, or if the person had been shunned by the family, this task may often be avoided.	Mourners of a death by suicide, drug use or a lifestyle viewed as socially unacceptable may lack family and community support for talking about the deceased with fondness and affection, or talking about the deceased at all.[155]
4. Relinquish old attachments to the deceased and to the old world - The nature of God may come into question, and the "old world" might include relinquishing a previously-held God image. This transition may or may not be met with family or community support.	Lora wondered if her 30 year-old son, who'd died from AIDS, would go to hell for being gay. Recognizing that this doctrine may not be viable, she questioned the idea of eternal damnation in her weekly bible study group, where she was chastised for questioning the group's interpretation of scripture.

5. Readjust to the new world without forgetting the old--In the past, God may have been seen as protector/ punisher, but the new world may introduce new beliefs. One may resist these changes, or experience pressure from church and community to remain in the old world.	When Rae's young child became ill and died, despite the fervent prayers of her family, church congregation and home school group, her belief in the power of God to answer prayers was challenged, and she began to explore alternative religions, which was met with disapproval from her friends, family and church.
6. **Reinvest energy**--Shifting focus away from the past and/or the lost loved one may feel as if one is no longer being loyal to the person or to the old world. In a religious framework, a shift in spiritual attitudes may suggest worshipping false gods or violating religious creeds.	Steve's daughter and son were killed together in a car crash. Steve said, "I only asked God for one thing in my life…to keep my children safe." He is now angry at God for not honoring this request. Instead of allowing a new image of God to emerge, he focuses his energy on anger at the old god.

Rando also identifies the following high-risk factors for complicated grief.[156] It is interesting to note that religious belief is not included in this list:

RANDO'S HIGH-RISK FACTORS	SELECTED EXAMPLES
Sudden or unexpected death (especially when traumatic, violent or mutilating).	Murder, suicide, natural disaster, war.

Death from a lengthy illness.	A caregiver may feel guilty for experiencing a sense of relief after the death occurs.
The mourner's perception of the death as preventable.	School shootings, drug overdose, suicide, or belief that the caregiver for a seriously ill person could have done more to prevent the death.
A pre-morbid relationship with the deceased that was markedly angry, ambivalent or dependent.	Death of an abusive spouse or a loved one from whom the mourner was estranged. Or an overly-dependent relationship that one "can't live without."
Prior or current mourner liabilities, including (a) unaccommodated losses and/or stresses and (b) mental health problems of the bereaved.	Unresolved grief from prior losses, loss of self/identity, unfinished business with the deceased, diminished capacity for understanding the loss.
The mourner's lack of social support when the deceased's lifestyle choices are perceived as socially unacceptable.	Grieving an abortion, death by drug overdose or suicide, or the death of someone killed while perpetrating a criminal act.
Loss of a child.	All of the above.

Examples of Complicated Grief

In my 2014 book, *Turning the Corner on Grief Street*, I recounted some of the responses I received to a message I posted in a bereavement-focused Facebook group about how to "turn the corner" on acute grief and find peace in life again. The majority of the group members were inspired by what I said, but some were offended by the suggestion that recovery is possible for bereaved parents, who, in their opinion, would "never recover." Many of those responses were indicative of complicated grief, as evidenced in the following excerpts from that discussion (names have been changed):

From Karen:
I'm sorry, but I refuse to believe that my precious son was meant to die. Children are not supposed to die before their parents.

From Doris:
I don't care about spiritual growth. I just want my daughter back. All this talk is a bunch of crap and you only say this because you are denying your own pain. Wouldn't you give anything to have your son back with you?

From Joan:
Terri, did you lose a child? I don't think so. Or if you did, your child was not a big priority for you. I'm a resident of grief street, so what?

From Don:
What kind of mother are you Terri? You are saying that it's OK with you that your son died and that you accept it completely? I will NEVER accept that my child died. All I want is to have him back here with me. Why wouldn't you want that? What's wrong with you?

From Karen:
The fact that I am still sad and angry after five years, according to you, is a failure. How dare you say this to me! I will grieve any way I want to for as long as I want to, and I don't need spiritual "teachers" to tell me I'm doing it wrong.

From Anne:
I would trade everything and anything to have my child back.

From Don:
So you're saying that life is all about pain and conflict? Don't you know anything about positive thinking? Pain is negative and should be avoided.

In another example that illustrates behaviors and attitudes related to complicated grief, I recently gave a presentation at a chapter meeting for a national grief support group. After my talk, one of the attendees -- a man I will call Richard -- told me this story:

> My son was murdered six years ago. I think it's important for people to know that such things happen and that life is unfair, so wherever I go, I tell people about my son. When I go to the grocery store or the bank, and the clerk says, "Have a nice day," I tell them that I never have a nice day because my son was murdered. When they reply with, "I'm so sorry," I say, "Thank you, but you'll never understand until it happens to your own child." That's how I cope with my grief. I'm angry, and I intend to stay that way.[157]

It was hard to decide what was most disturbing about his comments; his determination to remain angry, or his need to project his pain onto strangers by inviting them to envision their own children being killed. I acknowledged that his anger was understandable. But I also suggested (gently) that the decision to *remain* angry to that degree is a choice, and there are other options that could be explored. His answer was, "I'm not interested in other options. This is how I *want* to feel. Anger *is* my choice."

Another example comes from "Sam" (we'll meet him again later in this chapter). Sam's toddler son died in a tragic car accident, and when I met Sam three years later, he was obsessed with the idea that God could return his son to him if he prayed hard enough. He went to the child's grave every day to bargain with God and wrestle with Satan to reverse what had happened and return his son to life.

These examples illustrate maladaptive responses to loss that suggest a diagnosis of complicated grief (yes, it *is* a diagnosable condition). In a 2003 study of prolonged grief reactions in widowed adults, psychiatry professor Mardi Horowitz and his research team found empirical criteria that could characterize complicated grief as a diagnosable mental disorder. Their study addressed the debate about whether "prolonged and turbulent" grief responses are pathological enough to be included in *The Diagnostic and Statistical Manual of Mental Disorders of the American Psychiatric Association* (DSM). The researchers concluded that seven possible symptoms could potentially serve as diagnostic criteria for a specific disorder.[158] These symptoms included:

1. Unbidden memories or intrusive fantasies related to the lost relationship.

2. Strong spells or pangs of severe emotion related to the lost relationship.

3. Distressingly strong yearnings or wishes that the deceased were there.

4. Feelings of being far too much alone or personally empty.

5. Excessively staying away from people, places or activities that remind the subject of the deceased.

6. Unusual levels of sleep interference.

7. Loss of interest in work, social, caretaking, or recreational activities to a maladaptive degree.[159]

These recommendations contributed to a major change in the next edition of the DSM. In the previous edition, the criteria for diagnosing major depression contained an exception for bereaved individuals. It excluded their symptoms from being considered in a diagnosis of major depressive disorder, since those symptoms were typical of bereavement, and within normal limits. But that exclusion was removed in the new edition (DSM 5), so that extreme bereavement could now be diagnosed as a recognized disorder if the person is still experiencing these symptoms six months after the loss.

This is a controversial change. Some experts argue against it because it allows *normal* bereavement to be medicalized, which could encourage some practitioners to prescribe antidepressants or other medications as treatment. Others are in favor of the change because bereavement can often *lead to* clinical depression.[160]

How We Got Here: The Evolution of Contemporary Grief Theory

Sigmund Freud's 1913 essay *Mourning and Melancholia* formed the foundation of a "grief work" theory that remained in popular use by psychotherapists for decades. Freud proposed that the lengthy and ongoing process of grieving should ultimately result in emotional detachment from the lost object. This process was part of a dynamic in which one initially directs intense emotional energy toward the lost object or person. Over time, the griever strives to pull that energy away from the lost object in order to separate from the connective bonds, memories and feelings that cause pain, with the ultimate result being diminishment of the attachment.[161]

This model influenced therapists and grief theorists for nearly 50 years, until research methods were refined and assumptions about grief were challenged.[162] Rather than rooting grief studies exclusively in psychoanalysis, as social, cultural and religious attitudes began to shift the 1960s, so did interpretations of existing grief research. Ideas such as stage theories, the belief that all bereaved people experience distress, and the necessity of Freud-style grief work were questioned,[163] and these ideas were replaced with updated theories.

Today's researchers propose that the old grief work model does not address the full range of the grief experience or the various types of processing that can occur, and may only apply to grievers who are experiencing severe symptoms. Today it is generally agreed that detachment from the deceased is not the ultimate goal, but instead, healing occurs by creating a new relationship that integrates the deceased into the continuing life of the griever.[164]

Often, when teaching classes or workshops, I will ask attendees to tell me what they think the term "complicated grief" means. Their understanding of the term is usually either limited or non-existent, and it is quite common for someone to say, "All grief is complicated when you lose a child." Most will define it as a loss experience that contains multiple elements, for example, someone dies on the way to their wedding, or is murdered by a family member. They might also think that grief is "complicated" because the griever has so many other tasks to attend to, for example, a man grieving the death of his wife while raising young children on his own, or someone grieving the death of a parent while trying to complete a PhD. In these interpretations, grief is seen as "complicated" because there are mitigating factors or multiple responsibilities for the griever to manage. Because the phrase "it's complicated" has recently become a popular social media buzzword used everywhere from teenage Twitter posts to nightly news broadcasts, a correct understanding of complicated grief can get lost in translation.

Several of the people I've worked with -- especially those who'd lost children -- had either diagnosed themselves or been diagnosed by a professional as suffering from complicated mourning. Others were aware that their grief was chronic, but didn't think there was anything unusual about it. In fact, several in the latter group were quite defensive and protective of their "right to grieve any way I want to for as long as I want to," as evidenced by the Facebook comments noted earlier in this chapter. I've heard dozens of bereaved parents say, "I can't let go of the pain because the depth of my pain is equal to the depth of love I have for my child."

Resilience

Horowitz and his team defined normal grieving as the ability to tolerate distressing moods and turbulent thoughts with an eventual return to equilibrium. By contrast, complicated grief contains extremes that can impair functioning to the point where equilibrium is out of reach.[165] These two ends of a spectrum speak to an individual's capacity for *resilience.*

Grief researchers Margaret Stroebe and Henk Schut studied how bereaved individuals engage in a process that alternates between coping with the loss and making adjustments in their lives to adapt to that loss. They called it "the dual process model," which means that the griever's energy is constantly oscillating back and forth between two different states: *loss* orientation and *restoration* orientation.[166] Sometimes grievers are focused on the *loss*, experiencing sadness, longing, regret, loneliness and other loss-oriented emotions. At other times, grievers focus on *restoration*, by accepting the loss, normalizing daily activities, and adapting to the idea of a new future. When grief become complicated (as it did for Richard, Sam and many of the people in the Facebook discussion), the two processes are out of balance, with more focus on loss than on restoration.

The American Psychological Association defines *resilience* as "the process of adapting well in the face of adversity, trauma, tragedy, threats or significant sources of stress." These responses are not considered unusual or extraordinary, and should not necessarily be interpreted as a denial or suppression of pain.[167] It's also important to recognize that these responses can be influenced by the griever's cultural norms or religious beliefs. Dr. George Bonanno, a pioneering researcher in loss and trauma, observes that a griever's guilt feelings can be exacerbated by a belief in divine punishment, which contributes to complicated grief and increased pain.[168] Bonanno also notes that resilience is not well-supported in the modern Western way of grieving,[169] and when bereaved people show "only minor and transient disruptions in their ability to function," psychologists sometimes find it to be an unusual or even pathological response.[170]

Selected Case Vignettes

In this section I will briefly describe selected cases from sources that include my experience as a chaplain, anecdotal stories from students and clients, cases shared with me by colleagues, and posts from the three Facebook groups I manage. These stories give examples of toxic theology and its impact on an individual's ability to cope with loss in a healthy way. The names and identifiable details have been changed.

Case Example 1: Gerald[171]

Gerald was raised in a Pentecostal church in a small southern town. He was not allowed to socialize outside the church community, nor did he have access to radio, television or secular reading material. Even Christian music and religious television programming was forbidden. Gerald was home-schooled, and for as long as he can recall, he was taught that only the people within his insulated religious community were saved, and everybody outside was going to hell, unless they could be converted. He recalls listening to sermons in church and lectures from his family about demons and burning for eternity. He now sees this community as an extremist religious cult.

Gerald's younger sister was sexually abused by their grandfather and also by other male church members, as were other girls in the community, including Gerald's mother.

When Gerald got older and it was discovered that he was gay, the community attributed it to demonic possession, and multiple exorcisms were performed. Demonic possession was believed to be the reason for any behavior that did not conform with the community's rigid expectations.

Gerald was able to escape the church as a young adult, but at age 50, he still struggles with guilt and images of God as a punishing parent. Throughout his adult life he felt that God was punishing him for every "bad thought" he'd have, and for his "sinful behaviors." He has struggled to establish a functional life for himself, but has been unable to establish a fulfilling career or a stable intimate relationship. When a job would be lost, or a relationship ended, Gerald could not process the loss without feeling that the loss was a punishment from God.

Case Example 2: Lorrainna[172]

At age 11 Lorrainna was removed from her family home after being repeatedly raped by her stepfather. She was sent to live with her grandmother, who belonged to a Jehovah's Witness sect that ignores sexual abuse claims by relying on the requirement in Deuteronomy 19:15 that there must be at least two witnesses in order to convict someone of a crime.[173]

The grandmother did not want Lorrainna to have any sort of counseling, because her church would see it as disobedience to the law that required witnesses to the abuse. Eventually the grandmother did allow Lorrainna to see a therapist, but hid this fact from her religious community.

Case Example 3: Carol Ann[174]

Carol Ann was removed from the family home at nine years old after having been sexually abused by family members and friends of the family. She was placed in foster care and began receiving counseling. She had tremendous anger, but her foster parents believed that anger was a sin. Whenever Carol Ann expressed her anger, she was told that the anger was coming from the devil and she must fight against it and remain composed so as not to give Satan any power.

Case Example 4: Donna[175]

Donna's only child Julianna died from leukemia at age nine when Donna was in her early 40s. Donna faithfully attended bible study groups and church services. Although she was open-minded and tentatively explored different religious views, she felt "locked in" to Christian doctrine and found it difficult to shake the idea that Julianna's death was her punishment for having an abortion two decades earlier. She believed that God took Julianna in exchange for the child she aborted. She continued attending church and bible study, but found herself increasingly attracted to other theologies, an attraction that added to her guilt for not being faithful to her religious tradition.

Case Example 5: Sam[176]

Sam lost his toddler son in a car accident. His wife -- under the influence of alcohol -- was driving the car, and the child was not in a car seat. Sam visited the boy's grave daily, where he prayed, begged and bargained with God to bring his son back. He believed that God could provide this miracle, because Satan had caused the death, and therefore God could reverse it.

Case Example 6: Doug[177]

For the past five years, Doug and his wife Amy have been running a local chapter of a national support organization for bereaved parents. They report that none of the parents in their group are functioning normally five or more years after their loss. They both feel that all the people in their group -- and all the bereaved parents they've ever met -- have complicated grief. Neither Doug nor Amy have any training in psychology or counseling. They got involved with the group after the death of their 12 year-old son Andrew five years ago.

Doug recalls that several times over the years. Andrew had casually mentioned that he didn't think he would live into adulthood. Although Doug and Amy were disturbed by hearing this, when it turned out that Andrew *did* die at a young age, Doug and Amy believed that God had been preparing them for this plan, and this provided some comfort during the first few months after Andrew's death.

Doug says that he and Amy are both "faith-filled Christians," but despite the temporary comfort they experienced, over time, as the reality of the loss set in, Doug became angry at God. In his words, "I was still going to church, so I didn't turn away from God completely, but I didn't trust him anymore, and I blamed him for what happened. It made me question God's love. How can he love me and allow me to experience this much pain? I not only lost my son, but also my faith in God. I was suicidal. I still am sometimes. Many bereaved parents are."

Case Example 7: Ursula[178]

After the death of her infant daughter from a heart condition, Ursula fell into a deep depression. Her marriage had always been unhappy, and without a child, she could see no reason to stay with her abusive husband. But when she told her parents that she wanted to leave, they told her that divorce angers God, and if she left, she would go to hell.

She stayed in the marriage, but became more severely depressed, and her parents insisted that she see a Christian psychologist. In their first session, the psychologist asked Ursula about her relationship with the church. When Ursula told the psychologist that she'd left the church years before and wanted nothing more to do with it, the psychologist told her that the death of the baby was God's punishment for her leaving the church.

5

Rejecting Toxic Doctrines

Cognitive scientist Dr. Daniel Dennett says, "It is time for us to put religion under the microscope and subject it to multidisciplinary research."[179] Because religion affects almost every aspect our lives, and perhaps most importantly, it affects our search for meaning, religious research is too important to ignore,[180] and ignorance has no benefit. Dennett recognizes however, that this sort of scrutiny would meet with tremendous resistance, because if religion is examined closely, the spell would be broken, and so would the hearts of countless people.[181]

If this scrutiny is to be multidisciplinary, then perhaps the best place to start is with the theologians themselves.

Theologian and scholar Matthew Fox spent 34 years in the Catholic Dominican order before being expelled for questioning the doctrine of original sin. Today he is a leading voice in a movement for making Christianity more progressive and more relevant to contemporary life. Now an Episcopal priest, Fox suggests that we replace the idea of original sin with a more life-affirming, less-threatening concept called *original blessing*. He poses the question,

"How is religion to be an agent of transformation if religion itself is not transformed?"[182]

Following in the footsteps of Martin Luther, Fox proposed a "new reformation" in 2005 when he published *95 Theses or Articles of Faith for a Christianity for the Third Millennium* and tacked it to the door of the Wittenberg church where Luther displayed his original 95 Theses in the 16th century.[183] Fox's document rejected concepts like original sin, eternal punishment and a human-style god who has an opinion about how we behave, and replaced them with a god that is not tied to doctrines. Here's a sampling from Fox's 95 theses:

> **Thesis #4:** The notion of a punitive, all-male God is contrary to the full nature of the Godhead, who is as much female and motherly as it is masculine and fatherly.

> **Thesis #11:** Religion is not necessary, but spirituality is.

> **Thesis #55:** God speaks today as in the past through all religions and all cultures and all faith traditions, none of which is perfect or an exclusive avenue to truth, but all of which can learn from each other.

> **Thesis #62:** The universe does not suffer from a shortage of grace, and no religious institution is to see its task as rationing grace. Grace is abundant in God's universe.

Fox describes our current understanding of Christianity as "a religious tradition that begins with sin and centers almost exclusively around redemption from sin." He suggests that we redefine sin as "any action that injures creation and disrupts harmoniousness."[184] He also offers an alternative to the idea of salvation… instead of striving for an unattainable perfection and dividing the world into saved vs. unsaved, we can rise to the understanding that *all* experience is holy, and we can see God's presence as much in suffering as we see it in joy. We accomplish this by learning to view ourselves as part of an original *blessing* rather than an original *sin*.[185] This blessing is the very self-awareness that Adam and Eve were forbidden to have. As the myth tells us, when they ate the forbidden fruit, their awareness did increase. Sadly, church doctrine cast that as a rebellious sin rather than a momentous step forward in human evolution.

Fox's views speak to a new definition of the divine based on inclusion, ethics and love (both brotherly and universal). For Christians, this can still include everything that Jesus taught, but does not have to include the guilt-and-unworthiness doctrines established by the organized church. Adam and Eve becoming self-aware represents the cognitive development of the human race. Imagine how different our spiritual lives might be if we saw that as a gift instead of a crime.

Episcopal priest Barbara Brown Taylor tells the story of her experience attending a Native American ceremony in which she was at first extremely fearful and uncomfortable, but then came to admire the authentic connection to spirit that she witnessed there. She was impressed by the singing and dancing, the absence of books, the inclusive sense of community, and the emphasis on experiencing direct encounters with God.[186] Her spiritual journey eventually led her to a theology that did not depend on the trappings of the church. She learned that faith is not defined by certainty in what one believes, but by trust in one's awareness of the divine, which is more faithful than certainty.[187] She asks, "What if people were invited to church to tell what they already know of God instead of to learn what they're supposed to believe? What if the job of the church is to move people out the door instead of trying to keep them in?"[188]

Square Pegs in Round Holes

In his book *Love, Violence and The Cross*, Dr. Gregory Love critiques the doctrine of substitutionary atonement (the idea that Jesus bore humanity's sins, and his death constituted atonement for all of us), while at the same time lamenting its loss from contemporary Christianity. He states, "Today the Christian church is losing this center, and with it, the good news that the end of divine-human estrangement... has been accomplished in the work of Jesus."[189]

He identifies this work as the "central Christian assertion,"[190] but also points out its many flaws, including how the theory of substitutionary atonement justifies abuse and violence by glorifying the suffering of the innocent.[191] He wrestles mightily with this doctrine in a precarious balancing act in which he attempts to remain faithful to the teachings of the church while questioning the validity of its central assertion.[192]

Similarly, progressive pastor Rob Bell also takes aim at major teachings, in particular, the notion of eternal damnation in hell and the image of God as a cruel punisher. In his book *Love Wins*, he reminds readers that the concept of hell in the afterlife isn't biblical,[193] and also says that the image of God as a violent taskmaster is "psychologically crushing."[194]

But despite his disagreement with these teachings, Bell identifies strongly as a Christian, and while he helps us deconstruct the unhelpful beliefs, he retains most of Christianity's essential theology... that Jesus is the only path to God. He tells us that because Jesus is one with God, we can be one with God too, by going through Jesus as a conduit.[195] In Bell's words, this will allow God to "rescue us from death, sin and destruction."[196]

Although both authors attempt to present a critical analysis, they both end up bringing us right back where we started; to a theology that characterizes humanity as innately flawed and in need of rescue. Dr. Love substantiates this view when he says:

> "God could quite justly have abandoned us to our fate. He could have left us alone to reap the fruit of our wrongdoing and to perish in our sins. It is what we deserved. But he did not. Because he loved us, he came after us in Christ. He pursued us even to the desolate anguish of the cross, where he bore our sin, guilt, judgment and death."[197]

Bell and Love are passionate about the dangers of doctrines like eternal damnation and substitutionary atonement, but they are still talking about God as a humanized father figure and judge; an image that does not fit in to a vision of progressive theology.

Trying to match doctrine and dogma with actual human experience is like trying to put a square peg into a round hole. The square peg is a belief in divine reward and punishment. The round hole is the way life actually works. By the time most of us are adults, it has been proven to us over and over again that the good are not necessarily rewarded and the bad are not necessarily punished. We see no evidence of the punishment/reward model in real life. That's why the only way the emerging church could control human behavior with the threat of divine punishment was to locate it in the afterlife, where it could not be proven or disproven.

Instead of grappling endlessly with doctrines and beliefs that are difficult to understand and even more difficult to apply to daily living, why not simply reject those ideas entirely?

United Methodist minister Roger Wolsey says, "The notions that either God had to lethally punish his son for the sins that the rest of humanity commits, or that Jesus is our proxy/substitute for a necessary and required Divine transaction are of course abhorrent and reprehensible to progressive Christians."[198] Bishop Spong put it more bluntly when he declared, "The idea of Jesus dying for your sins has to go." He explains that seeing Jesus as a rescuer is a form of magical thinking that allows the church to use guilt as an imperative for conversion,[199] and that moving theism aside would free us to explore spirituality in new ways.[200] Matthew Fox echoes Spong's sentiments by stating that "we must move from theism to panentheism so that we can find God in everything, and everything in God."[201]

Spirituality vs. Religion

As more and more people abandon traditional religious structures and opt to identify as "spiritual but not religious," notions of suffering, sin and redemption are changing. The first time I heard the term "Spiritual But Not Religious" was on an internet dating site in 2007, in the section where users check a box to indicate their religious preferences. The term has since become its own theological framework, sparking research and commentary by theologians worldwide. It has even earned an acronym: *SBNR*.

Theology professor Linda Mercadante, in studying people who identify as SBNR, found that most of her interviewees did not see death as a "hostile force" or an enemy,[202] and that belief in an afterlife is more than just a choice between heaven and hell.[203] Similarly, Drescher's findings showed that the same population is not concerned with "future-oriented expectations traditionally associated with salvation or various other afterlife schemas,"[204] and in order to be a good person, it is not necessary to believe in a god that rewards and punishes.[205] Current data from the Pew Research studies on America's religious demographics reveal a similar picture. Traditional religious beliefs have given way to a population that identifies as religiously unaffiliated; a group that now makes up 23% of the adult population in the U.S.[206]

Retired Harvard Divinity professor Dr. Harvey Cox explains this shift by identifying three evolving periods in the evolution of Christian thinking. The first period, which he calls "the age of faith," began with Jesus and his original followers, whose faith launched the religious movement that would soon experience explosive growth. Being a Christian had one simple definition... follow Jesus in the work that he had begun.

The second period Cox refers to as "the age of belief," which emerged with the formation of the early church, when belief in doctrines, creeds and catechisms became the foundation for being a Christian rather than faith in Jesus and his message. These teachings were focused on stories *about* Jesus rather than messages *from* him.[207] When Constantine declared Christianity to be the official religion of the Roman empire in the 4th century, the age of belief took hold and kept its grip for more or less the next 1500 years.[208]

But now, Cox says, we are entering a third period that he calls "the age of spirit," in which it is the direct experience of spirit that connects us to God rather than doctrines and beliefs.[209] In today's world, the influence of Asian spirituality and mystical practices from other cultures has made these kinds of experiences more accessible, despite the objections of the church. As Cox points out, on any given day you can find Catholic monks meditating cross-legged in India, Benedictines teaching centering prayer, and Tai Chi or yoga classes taught in church basements. All of these practices were not that long ago viewed with suspicion by church authorities.[210]

Dr. Duane Bidwell, in his book *When One Religion Isn't Enough,* uses the term "religious multiplicity,"[211] to describe people who are shaped by or bonded with more than one religious community simultaneously. He describes himself as both a Buddhist and a Christian, seeing Jesus as his savior and Buddha as his teacher.[212] In the world of the internet, where information about world cultures and diverse religious views can be accessed instantly with the click of a mouse, the boundaries between ethnic groups, nations and thought systems are shifting. Bidwell points out that these fluid boundaries --whether geographical, existential, sociopolitical or theological -- attract seekers to "borderlands" where beliefs, traditions, practices, languages and cultural references mingle. One might choose what Bidwell calls a "dual religious citizenship,"[213] while others may embark on an open-ended exploration that evolves over time, without settling on any specific tradition.

Theologian Dr. Phillip Clayton points out that America's religious landscape today is a far cry from what it was in the 1950s, when a person's Christian or Jewish identity was key to defining who they were.[214] He cites Will Herberg's 1955 study, *Protestant, Catholic, Jew,* which stated that 95% of American people declared themselves to be either Protestants, Catholics, or Jews.[215]

It is a very different story today. The 2014 Pew Research Religious Landscape study concluded that "The Christian share of the U.S. population is declining, while the number of U.S. adults who do not identify with any organized religion is growing."[216] As Putnam and Campbell's 2010 study of religiosity in America noted, most of us now *choose* our religious preferences rather than *inheriting* them, and "roughly half of white Americans have departed from their parents' religious stance, either through switching to a different religious tradition or through lapsing into religious indifference."[217]

Cox identified what may be the pivotal point of departure for most people when he said, "People are drawn more to the experiential than to the doctrinal elements of religion."[218] With experiential resonance, one senses a personal, numinous, mystical interaction with the spiritual realm, as opposed to simply parroting doctrines and narratives that have been promoted by church, community and culture.

On the other end of the spectrum, the idea of personal revelatory experience is in stark opposition to the views of conservative pastor Rev. Lillian Daniel, who believes that we should not be allowed to come up with our own "human-invented god."[219] But aren't *all* gods human-invented? And shouldn't the spiritual quest, as described in Unitarian Universalist Principle #4, be all about "a free and responsible search for truth and meaning?"[220]

For many Americans, a free and responsible search for truth and meaning led directly to the birth of the SBNR movement. Mercadante observed that SBNR thinking "relocates authority from external to internal."[221] Among her study subjects, the term "spirituality" was commonly referred to as an interior life of faith, while "religion" contained a communal or organizational component.[222] As Drescher described, the SBNRs are more interested in *being* than in *believing*, and do not require a statement of faith or a lifelong commitment to something that by its very nature is dynamic and changeable.[223] Instead of bowing down to an all-powerful man-in-the-sky, the SBNR population is looking for something more life-affirming and more nurturing than what Bishop Spong describes as "a barbaric god and a world full of humans who are little more than guilt-filled creatures."[224]

The ambiguity of a spiritual rather than a religious outlook can be uncomfortable for those steeped in creed-bound or bible-based religious views. Spirituality (vs. religiosity) can be perceived as dissent, and dissent has traditionally been discouraged by the church.[225] But consider the fact that Jesus himself was a dissenter. Even though he followed the customs of his Jewish heritage, his perspective (as we understand it), was not perfectly aligned with the beliefs held by the followers of Yahweh. While the god of the Hebrew scriptures was exclusively on the side of the Israelites,[226] the god described by the Christian gospels loved and accepted everybody, regardless of social status, nationality, religious community or gender.[227] Jesus shook up the popular faith of the day by challenging social norms and images of God that no longer served the population; a shake-up that forged the foundation of Christianity.

SBNRs do not set out to challenge traditional faith, but instead, invite the faithful to find deeper meaning through teachings and practices that have more relevant, more personal application in today's world. But just like those who found Jesus' message to be threatening to the status quo, not everybody sees the SBNR movement as a positive one. Rev. Lillian Daniel is one of today's most prominent voices speaking out against those who identify as spiritual but not religious. Her scornful analysis of the SBNR population goes so far as to suggest that the unaffiliated or un-churched are socially and politically apathetic, and rather than getting involved in humanitarian causes, they simply sit around "feeling lucky for their good fortune" rather than trying to help others.[228] She refers to the SBNR view of the divine as a "cheap god of self-satisfaction and isolation."[229] Her disdain for SBNRs reaches new heights when she sarcastically refers to the children of SBNR parents as "junior theologians" and "theological geniuses" for thinking that God is a rainbow.[230]

Relative to her scathing critique of what is popularly referred to as "New Age theology," the following chart -- published by a Christian website -- compares New Age beliefs with Christian beliefs. Even though the website is strongly fundamentalist Christian (their statement of faith says, "The Bible is verbally inspired by the Holy Spirit, wholly true, without error in the original canon of 66 books"), it offers a surprisingly even-handed assessment of what could be considered SBNR cosmology and theology.[231]

CONCEPTS OF...	NEW AGE/OCCULT/ EASTERN	CHRISTIANITY
Man	Basically good. Inherently divine. Part of God.	Created in God's image but also has a sinful nature.
God	Impersonal force. Creative energy or principle. Manifests as nature or various gods.	Personal living God, sovereign ruler of the universe, the only living true God.

Earth	Sacred. Living organism. Has consciousness. Assisted by earth spirits.	Created by God for His own purposes to ultimately glorify Him.
Salvation	By works: Liberation from this life by evolving through re-incarnation. Performance of good works. Enlightenment by following a guru, through meditation, in special rituals or laws. Enlightenment through realization of one's divine nature. No need for salvation.	By grace: Through faith in the death of Christ to pay for our sins and the resurrection to give us His life.
Evil	Does not exist or is defined as ignorance... Part of a dualistic oneness composed of good/evil (Taosim & Yin-Yang) so that in reality there is no good or evil.	Evil is rebellion against God's will through man's sinful nature and through Satan.

Jesus Christ	An enlightened teacher like Buddha. A man who achieved "Christ consciousness," and awareness of man's innate divine nature, which all can achieve. Avatar of the Age of Pisces. A magician. Graduate of esoteric mystery schools.	The 2nd Person of the Trinity. God's only begotten Son (same nature as God). The promised Messiah. The God-man who perfectly obeyed the Father, enabling him to be the sacrifice for all sin by His death & shedding of blood on the cross. The only Mediator between God & man.

Christian historian Diana Butler Bass defines spiritual awakening as "the work of learning to see differently."[232] The SBNRs are doing that work, and their new way of seeing is paving the way to new ways of knowing God, which creates opportunities to perceive loss as something other than punishment.

"Pain that is not transformed will be transmitted"

-- RICHARD ROHR

6

Healing and Restoration

In the documentary film, *Active Shooter: America Under Fire,*[233] the father of a child killed in a school shooting talked about learning to live with his overwhelming grief. In six words he summed it up beautifully:

"You learn to carry it better."

This is a healthy and hoped-for outcome in the process of restoring balance and well-being after a trauma or profound loss. However, with complicated grief, the griever does *not* learn to carry it better. Instead of alternating between loss-orientation and restoration-orientation, the griever focuses almost exclusively on the loss. Resilience seems out of reach.

The American Psychological Association identifies certain inner qualities that may contribute to a person's capacity for resilience.[234] These qualities include:

- The capacity to make realistic plans and take steps to carry them out.

- A positive view of yourself and confidence in your strengths and abilities.

- Skills in communication and problem solving.
- The capacity to manage strong feelings and impulses.

When an individual suffering from complicated grief has limited abilities in any of these areas, throwing a religious conflict into the mix can make it more difficult. To begin looking at some innovative new (and sometimes ancient) tools that can help establish balance between loss and restoration, let us first look at traditional therapeutic approaches and why they may not necessarily be effective.

Alternatives to Counseling

Because grieving is a natural process and not a psychological disorder, when a bereaved individual seeks counseling for normal (non-complicated) grief, counseling may provide very little relief. While acknowledging that research methods in this area are in need of improvement, grief researchers Jordan and Neimeyer pointed out that the conventional approach to grief counseling is based on a *medical treatment* model in which a clinician diagnoses a patient and then treats the patient for a specific condition. They concluded that this model may have only limited use for working with bereavement, and found that there is little scientific evidence for the efficacy of grief counseling in this format.[235]

In traditional settings where grievers might seek counseling, the medical model tends to prevail, often because providers aren't specifically trained in bereavement care.[236] Church-based counselors may lack sufficient training or experience in psychology (grief theory in particular), or may only be able to offer support within the framework of religious doctrines. Conversely, secular counselors may have little or no familiarity with spiritual care. In addition, across the board, both secular and pastoral counselors may not be familiar with alternative or multi-cultural modalities that draw on practices such as guided imagery, meditation, breath work, dream work, body work and sacred ceremony.

Within my own professional sphere, as I become more involved in working with the bereaved, I consistently find that many of the people I interact with have been going to counseling or support groups for years, but are still unable to find peace. Recalling Doug's statement from Chapter 4, he perceived that all the people in his grief group -- and all the bereaved parents he'd ever met -- have complicated grief. Even Doug, who has no training in counseling, could see that they aren't progressing in their healing.

If the medical model has limited use, and if traditional providers lack training in either bereavement or spiritual care, and if groups like Doug's are moderated by peer supporters rather than professionals, what constitutes a truly *effective* intervention for complicated grief?

In 2014 I addressed this gap by creating a workshop called *Grief as a Mystical Journey.*[tm] It was originally designed for bereaved individuals, but has expanded over the years to include training for mental health professionals. The workshop content draws upon teachings and practices from a variety of multi-cultural and inter-spiritual sources that introduce participants to diverse views of suffering and healing. At least 60% of the workshop contains interactive, experiential group processes, many of which are designed to help participants move into a more fluid spiritual landscape that does not contain toxic imagery.

To encourage reliance on one's own inner resources while supporting theological flexibility, participants are invited to explore the following:

- Views of suffering from different spiritual traditions
- Loss and trauma as a source of spiritual and emotional growth
- Suffering as purposeful rather than random or punitive
- Ancient and contemporary rituals for working with grief

Not all the participants are coping with religious issues, but the workshop also includes tools and learning objectives that address toxic religion along with grief work in general:

- Identifying religious beliefs that may be complicating the grief process.

- Unique therapeutic tools not ordinarily found in traditional counseling or grief group settings, including working with sacred symbolism, creative ritual, family dynamic mapping, community grieving, interactive group processes, guided meditation and inter-spiritual mystical practices.

- Shifting the griever's focus toward inner transformation and away from external events.

- Multi-cultural practices from a variety of spiritual paths, with inter-religious content and alternatives to doctrinal limitations that can contribute to complicated mourning.

- Personal rituals to replace traditional rituals that may have become meaningless.

- New spiritual resources beyond those of an inherited religion.

- Techniques for healing in community rather than in isolation.

- New forms of prayer that do not include disempowering imagery.

- New language to describe mystical concepts.

- Re-framing the way a relationship with the divine can look and function.

In addition to psychological processes such as art and music therapy, the workshop also incorporates spiritual practices drawn from a variety of world religions and cultures. Parts of the workshop involve sacred song, which includes a Hindu chant (*Aud Guray Nameh*); a Hebrew chant (intoning the word *Ruah*); and grief laments from the Celtic Pagan tradition. We create altars called "stations of the heart" (based on the Catholic tradition of stations of the cross); and we perform a Peruvian shamanic prayer ceremony called a *Kintu*. There's something for everybody.

These deeply-felt processes invite us into a meditative state where we find our spiritual center and infuse the ceremonial actions with personal meaning. These activities help release rigid adherence to beliefs and traditions that have proven unhelpful, and replaces them with a more practical, more personal means for allowing grief to lead to strength and wisdom rather than chronic sadness.

One particularly effective tool for those who are struggling with religious issues is a fascinating little exercise that is a spin-off on the "telephone game" that many of us played as children. In this schoolyard game, a group of children form a line, and the child at the front of the line whispers a phrase to the child next to her. Then that child whispers it to the next, and the next child whispers it to the next, and so on down the line. At the end of the game, the last child to hear the phrase recites it to the group, and it is barely recognizable as the original story told by the first child in line.

In the workshop, I use this exercise to illustrate how mythologies, scriptural narratives and traditions were handed down and interpreted over the centuries. It's an informative, lively and entertaining way to learn how to use discernment and intuition when interpreting religious writings. Here's how it works:

- I remove three people from the room and read a Native American creation story to the group that remains.

- I then bring the first person back into the room and have an audience member repeat the story to her.

- Then the second person returns, and the first person repeats the story to him, and so on.

- Finally, I read the original story again to help everybody recognize how much it had changed.

In the 20 minutes it takes to complete the exercise, the key details of the story are lost. Names are changed or omitted, and personal biases are inserted. Important time frames, the placement of physical objects, the motivation behind the characters' actions and the sequence of events are drastically changed. This happens in a group of 30 people with four storytellers in a span of only 20 minutes. Imagine what happens over hundreds or thousands of years after numerous translations, ideological shifts and personal spins are attached to the stories by thousands of storytellers.

Important to note... when I conduct this exercise, I intentionally choose the oldest person, the youngest person, and a non-native English speaker, because this is how the original religious stories were handed down, translated from language to language and transmitted orally from elders to children. These teachings were also carried across ever-changing political and linguistic borders, and were frequently altered according to the personal preferences of the storyteller. By the time writing and printing became possible, the original stories were altered beyond recognition.

Restoring Spiritual Health

For many grievers, a minister or priest may be a primary source for counseling and comfort. But often, members of the clergy lack specific training in grief counseling and are not familiar with current research in bereavement care. For example, Elizabeth Kubler Ross' "five stages of grief" are still referenced by many mental health care providers, even though the stage theory has long since been abandoned in favor of newer ideas focused on tasks rather than stages. Ministers who are not familiar with these contemporary trends in grief theory may not be able to provide adequate spiritual care.[237]

But even if a griever seeks solace exclusively from a religious source without regard to psychology or grief theory, many of our familiar religious practices fail to engage the soul at a deeper level. For example, rituals such as funeral services, holiday customs, conventional liturgies and routine prayers are often generic and performed by rote, which some mourners may find lacking in meaning and personal relevance.

In Bonanno's exploration of grief practices around the world, he concluded that the way we grieve in the West underestimates our capacity to heal ourselves after an extremely difficult or traumatic event.[238] Modern Western thinking, steeped in a value system that places independence and self-reliance above collective experience, tends to see grieving as a private, individual process rather than a communal one.[239] Not only do we grieve alone, but by denying the reality of death,[240] we have become estranged from ancient practices that were designed to help us have a more personal relationship with the natural cycles of change and impermanence. As psychiatrist and grief expert Colin Murray Parkes points out, "We live in a world in which religion and the fundamental idea with which it deals -- birth, death and the meaning of life -- have been taken over by professionals, and quietly downgraded in personal significance."[241]

How did this happen?

Matthew Fox observes that we have lost our connection to the cosmos. Instead of invoking the energies of the sun and moon, the power of nature and the unseen forces of the universe that are so much a part of the birth/death experience, traditional Christian rituals focus primarily on scriptural narratives and religious doctrine. This is because, as Fox states, "The fall/redemption tradition does not trust the cosmos, and does not celebrate it."[242] To Fox's point, worshipping the sun, moon and stars is an abomination punishable by death in Deuteronomy 17:2-5.

In order to restore the sacred practices and the cosmic connection that has been lost, we can begin by exploring cultures and religions that may be unfamiliar to us, but can offer fresh inspiration and new spiritual direction. We can learn much from indigenous customs that have maintained a close relationship with the earth and the elements, and we can use those elements in our own spiritual practices.

Unique Approaches

In one of my graduate school counseling courses, we were given a set of scenarios and asked how we would address the client's spiritual crisis. The examples given here are creative approaches that might be taken when time-honored, conventional religious solutions fail to offer comfort and guidance:

Scenario #1

The priest at your church shares with you that he has been observing more addictive behaviors in his parishioners. He is beginning to believe that "we are an addictive culture," and insists that addiction is nothing more than sinful actions and willful gratification. Desire must be corralled in what amounts to a "spiritual battle." The priest asks for your feedback. How would you respond?

I would bear in mind that as priest, he is coming from a frame of reference that includes his own addictions... to doctrines, belief systems, images of God, personal biases and theories about human behavior. I would begin by asking him to examine those attachments and assumptions before passing judgment on others.

To help him reconcile his perception of addiction as sinful with his personal devotion to God, I might quote Gerald May's observation that we "displace our longing for God upon other things."[243] Bringing the experience of addiction within the realm of the holy might help him soften his harsh condemnation of the parishioners. Asking him to reconsider that stance would challenge him to embark on his own theological reflection.

If he was willing to reflect in that way, I would offer a view from a different theological angle that doesn't attribute negative behavior to sin, but allows for the fact that we are all spiritual beings on a growth path, and our "sins" are simply part of the learning curve. I would share with him that there are other ways of looking at "willful gratification," and I would suggest that the ego-centered actions of human beings are not necessarily evil, because they can be used as tools for transcendence. People struggling with addiction are seeking relief from their psychic and/or physical pain. The spiritual battle is a struggle to work with the attachments and response styles that cause that pain, which is a journey that can be honored rather than judged.

Scenario #2

A young mother describes worrying all the time and being caught up in negative thoughts. She mentioned that her childhood was "tough" and stated that she always felt "unworthy." She believes that Jesus does not want us to be anxious, but when she tries to fight her fears, the pessimism always wins. What approach might you take to help reduce her anxiety?

In order to address her immediate need for relaxation, I would start with meditation and visualization processes for calming the body. If she could learn to slow down the ongoing panorama of fearful, anxious thoughts, even for one or two seconds at a time while she focuses on breathing, she could develop an "observing self" that could manage those thoughts. By experiencing a few seconds in which she's not in an agitated state, the neuroplasticity of her brain would begin to learn that moments of peace *are* possible.

I would also explore her personal theology. Does she believe that she -- and all of humanity -- is unworthy? If so, I would try to help her see that such a belief, while it may be doctrinal, is unhelpful when trying to understand the human condition. In order to truly find peace, the concept of innate unworthiness is an impediment that needs to be shifted toward a new paradigm.

To begin that shift, I would help her find new language to describe her experience. She says that she tries to "fight" her fears, so I would suggest using a word that doesn't sound so aggressive. Because she believes that Jesus doesn't want us to have anxiety, the image of "fighting" may seem culturally or theologically inappropriate for her, and may only serve to increase her anxiety. I would try to help her learn how to perceive those thoughts not as enemies to be vanquished, but as messages from her own soul that reveal areas in need of love or healing. Instead of "fighting" them or trying to push them away, I would show her how to embrace them, honor them, and then gently *release* them. I would do this via a visualization process in which she sends the fearful thoughts to the light (or in her case, to Jesus) for healing, or releases them in a ceremony.

Scenario #3

A parishioner at your church was recently diagnosed with a terminal illness, and was told that she has 3-4 months to live. Her grief is felt most acutely vis-à-vis her two young daughters, whom "I will never see grow up, graduate from high school, become adults, get married and have children...." She wants to know what you think about suffering and acceptance. What would you say/not say to her?

I would share with this client and her family, the following processes for working with suffering and acceptance:

Allowing Assumptions to Shift

Much of what we experience when facing loss and trauma is the breaking down of familiar structures that make us feel secure and safe. This client is struggling with the assumption that life is supposed to unfold in a particular way, and that we should expect to watch our children grow up and have children of their own. But now she is now grappling with a new reality. In order to help her and her family navigate this massive shift and move toward acceptance, I would try to help them understand that reality is neither absolute nor predictable. In a theological context, that would include exposure to other theological, cosmological systems and practices for coping with pain and loss that extend beyond the parameters of her religious framework.

This would include an exploration of the client's image of God, and the cultural, religious and experiential references she uses for defining reality.[244] Depending on her willingness to investigate other views, I might familiarize her with the Buddhist perspective on suffering as a necessary part of spiritual growth vs. a Christian perspective that sees suffering as either random or punitive.

End-of-Life Communication Skills

The importance of honest, open communication with family members at end-of-life cannot be overstated. I would offer to facilitate a family meeting -- or a series of meetings -- in which the impending death can be discussed and specific plans can be made. Family members would be invited into a safe space in which they can express their grief and develop skills to help them communicate more effectively about their pain, their fear and their love. This would also provide a forum for asking any questions they might have about the death process, and assisting them in finding language that is comfortable (for example, using the words "death" and "dying" instead of euphemistic terms that make communication more cumbersome).

Meditation, Visualization and Ceremony

Once the family can move into a place where the death is not hidden in darkness and denial, they might be ready to start using a mindfulness meditation technique for tapping into a place of peaceful acceptance. By using this practice, the family members can be brought into alignment with present time rather than focusing on resentments from the past or fears about the future. I would also help the family create rituals and ceremonies to manage the energies of pain, sadness, guilt, regret and other powerful emotions.

The Importance of Ritual and Ceremony

When bereaved individuals seek psychological counseling or the support of a chaplain in a healthcare setting, it is rare to find non-traditional, "outside-the-box" rituals and ceremonies used as part of the therapeutic process. Most therapists and counselors are not specifically trained in bereavement work, and have even less familiarity with multi-cultural ceremonies for addressing grief. And while ministers and chaplains may be familiar with rituals from within their own faith traditions, they may not recognize that many of these rituals have lost their meaning for some followers.

Matthew Fox writes, "The grief in the human heart needs to be attended to by rituals and practices that, when practiced, will lessen anger and allow creativity to flow anew."[245]

The idea of *flowing anew* is beautiful, and exactly what rituals are designed to support. Grief and trauma are heavy burdens that if not properly addressed, can anchor themselves in the body, mind and spirit until they manifest as complicated mourning, illness, depression, addiction or suicide. Creative rituals can loosen that anchor and release us from a sense of hopelessness and despair.

But traditional, conventional rituals may not reach far enough to engage the deeper inner processes necessary for healing. As an example, the most common grief ritual in our culture is the funeral, which blends several types of rituals and symbols, including a processional (to represent walking from one reality to another), burial (which helps us recognize that the body is no longer viable), gathering in community (to support each other in collective loss), and acknowledgement of spiritual principles that help us find meaning (the soul continuing in an afterlife).

But after the funeral, after the friends stop calling and the casseroles stop showing up, those rituals essentially end, and a critical period in the healing process is ignored.

Dr. Kenneth Doka, senior consultant to the Hospice Foundation of America, suggests that rather than seeing a funeral as a one-time activity, we should develop new and continued rituals over time throughout the mourning process, which can extend the therapeutic value of a funeral or memorial service.[246] He also identifies various types of rituals that mark different milestones and serve different purposes -- such as rituals for continuity, transition, reconciliation or affirmation -- to meet the specific needs of the griever.[247]

Mayan shaman Martin Prechtel sees ritual as emerging from our tribal need to honor the natural transitions in life and the losses for which we grieve. These transitions are profound rites of passage that must be honored ritually and communally, so that the grief is "not left hanging, but is converted into ritual beauty and culture-supporting continuity."[248]

The healing value of ritual and ceremony is beginning to find its way into professional discourse among grief theorists and psychotherapists, but still has not established a strong presence in mainstream counseling practices. It interesting to note how easy it can be to confuse or conflate a ceremony with a therapeutic exercise. For example, in Neimeyer's "life imprint" process,[249] clients either verbalize or write a narrative about the imprint made on their lives by a deceased loved one. Similarly, Hochberg's[250] process of creating documentary audio or video to acknowledge a loved one's legacy is a beautiful tribute, as is Thompson's process of creating a commemorative flag to honor a fallen soldier.[251] These are useful therapeutic exercises, but in order to move the painful energy forward, the exercises must be accompanied by a *ritual action* that represents a shift in the way the energy of the loss is held -- emotionally and spiritually-- by the griever.

How can we ritualize these exercises in order to add a spiritual component to the work of healing? Below are some suggestions for how ritual and ceremony could be linked to the processes mentioned above to add a mystical dimension:

THERAPEUTIC EXERCISE	ACCOMPANYING RITUAL
Creating an audio or video tribute to a loved one at end-of-life (or for a deceased loved one)	To ritualize the narrative, mourners can take a long piece of yarn or string and slowly wind it into a ball while telling the story of the person's life. The completed ball, containing the stories, can be buried or cremated with the person,[252] or kept on the family altar until the one-year anniversary of the death, when it can be ceremonially released by burying it, putting it into a river, or tying it to a tree where the blessings can be carried by the wind, rain and sun.
Creating and sharing a written or spoken narrative	Burn the written piece (you can keep a copy if you wish) in a ceremonial fire to symbolically send a message to the deceased in the non-physical realm. If the imprint is negative (in the case of a conflicted relationship), the fire can be seen as purification for the painful memories, or the writing can be buried in the earth to be absorbed by the powerful and healing energy of nature. A spoken narrative can also be given to nature by speaking it into a stone and releasing the stone into a fire, a body of water, or burying it in the earth.

Designing/constructing a commemorative flag for a fallen soldier	Once the flag is constructed, it can be passed among the family members, as each whispers a prayer or blessing into it. It can then be kept on the family altar and used as a ceremonial object to acknowledge the deceased's birthday or death anniversary. At some point, if the family wishes, it could be placed into a river or burned as a symbol of releasing the relationship's old form to make way for the new one.

In order to begin incorporating transformative ritual into Western grieving practices, we have much to learn from the wisdom of other cultures. In Western society where autonomy and individualism are valued more than communal experience, it is challenging to create community rituals that will be acceptable across certain social and religious boundaries. We use a variety of strategies to distance ourselves from death in comparison to countries where war, poverty and political upheaval make death an everyday occurrence that cannot be ignored. Perhaps it is this acceptance that enables indigenous people to create rituals that not only help them cope with grief, but encourage community bonding. Sadly, in modern American life, we have turned the personal sacredness of ritual over to funeral directors and pastors, thus separating ourselves even further from the reality of death.[253]

The instinct to create ritual is innate and universal. It doesn't matter if the ritual makes offerings to the rain gods, the deities of the Hindu pantheon, the god of Abraham, the Native American

Great Spirit, or no gods at all. The purpose -- and the healing effect -- is equally powerful when the ritual is imbued with personal meaning. Grief rituals not only help us honor our losses, but also help us gently relinquish any unhealthy attachments we might be carrying in relation to those losses.

Many people ask what the difference is between ritual and ceremony. Although those terms are often used interchangeably, following are some helpful definitions.

It is generally understood that *rituals* are routines or customs that are repeated routinely, for example, having a Christmas tree every year and making a time-honored family recipe for Christmas dinner. A *ceremony* is a special spiritual process that is performed for a specific purpose with a specific intention, and can either be contained within a ritual, or stand on its own.

As an example, every year since 1990 I've hosted a Winter Solstice Ceremony and Celebration at my house to acknowledge the winter holiday season and honor the return of the light. The yearly gathering, with a pot luck, Christmas music and holiday merriment, is an annual event, which qualifies it as a *ritual*. But within that ritual, there is also a *ceremony*. In the ceremony, each person lights a candle on the altar and states their intention for bringing more light into their lives and into the world during the coming year. When that process is completed, each person writes on a slip of paper a description of an energy or an attachment they would like to release. We then gather around an outdoor fire where the strips of paper are burned to release those energies.

This ceremony, because we repeat it yearly as part of the Solstice celebration, could also be considered a ritual. But it is a ceremony as well, because it involves the symbolic representation of an intention or an action to create a shift in consciousness. Therefore, because "ceremony" and "ritual" cannot be clearly defined as completely separate concepts, they are not mutually exclusive, so the terms are frequently converged.

Rando observes that mourners who don't participate in appropriate rituals for acknowledging a death tend to have difficulty accepting the reality of the death,[254] which can be a symptom of complicated grief.[255] She discusses several psychological benefits of death and grief rituals in this excellent list:[256]

- **Acting out** (a purposeful behavioral expression of an internal thought or feeling).

- **Legitimization of emotional and physical ventilation** (ritual sanctions a mourner's expression of emotion).

- **Provision of symbols and outlets to focus thoughts, feelings and behaviors** (the use of symbol concretizes thought and affect, providing mourners with a tangible experience that would not be possible if abstractions alone were employed).

- **Rendering of control** (after undertaking a prescribed activity with symbolic meaning, a mourner often experiences emotional and physical release and a sense of increased manageability of emotions).

- **Delimitation of grief** (rituals can channel mourning into a circumscribed behavior with a distinct beginning and end).

- **Enhancement of appropriate connection to the deceased** (rituals can provide symbolic evidence of the deceased's continued existence in the life of the mourner).

- **Enablement of the Six Rs of Mourning**[257] (see page 72)

- **Learning through gained experience** (the active "doing" in ritual makes the reality of the loss more real and less abstract).

- **Provision of structure, form, and containment for confusing emotions** (rituals can contain emotions by offering protection against overpowering feelings and impulses, and can reduce anger).

- **Prescription of actions for dealing with emotional or social chaos** (rituals can reduce stress overload and provide grounding).

- **Provision of group experiences that allow kinship and social solidarity** (collective rituals facilitate social interaction to promote a mourner's re-integration into a social group).

- **Structuring celebrations, anniversaries and holidays** (appropriate rituals to commemorate occasions can be effective in tapping in to disturbing affects or cognitions associated with the special day).

There are no rules for what personal rituals and ceremonies should look like, but in my ceremonial work over the past ten years, I've identified these general guidelines:

- Rituals contain a mystical or metaphysical component, such as acknowledging spiritual energy, higher planes of consciousness or divine presence. This might involve sending a message to the spirit of a deceased loved one, or asking God, spirit guides, ancestors or angels to help with our healing.

- Rituals can be performed alone or in community. No institutional structure or professional facilitator is needed.

- Rituals are designed to shift energy from one condition to another. A ritual involving breath, movement or singing can release emotional pain from the body. A ritual in which the client draws a picture depicting a traumatic event and then burns that picture in a ceremonial fire helps to release disruptive or obsessive attachments to that image.

- Rituals work with symbolic representations of emotions and experiences. These symbols can include drawings, personal sacred objects, or objects from nature, such as stones or feathers. Moving or manipulating these objects in a ceremonial fashion (by burning in a fire, burying in the earth, purifying with water, etc.), symbolizes moving the pain from where it is "stuck" to a new location in spiritual space where it can be transmuted.

- Ritual gives words, symbols, objects and images to what is otherwise unspeakable, formless and invisible. It creates a bond between heaven and earth, and turns pain into power.[258]

Echoing my metaphysical description of ritual -- and Rando's psychological description -- Dr. Herbert Anderson, research professor in practical theology, identifies these characteristics of healing ritual from a Christian perspective:[259]

- Rituals connect people to communities of care and to the earth. The experience of community softens the isolation that lingering pain generates. God's healing is the work of restoring and redeeming the whole creation.

- Rituals make a correspondence between intense emotions or painful memories and words or images to express those emotions. The words and images of Christian rituals make explicit the link or correspondence between God's story and our stories.

- Rituals foster coherence of meaning in spite of inevitable mystery, because the deepest truths of life and faith are hidden in God.

Anderson also offers this interfaith, cross-cultural summary of how ritual and ceremony can provide healing while spanning the space between psychology and theology:

"Just as we use playful and poetic language to speak about the mystery of God, we use symbols, gestures, and song to point to the unspeakable in human pain, and make public what cannot be seen. Rituals express what cannot be captured in words...What makes human rituals so important in our lives generally, and so essential for healing, is that ritual is a vehicle for liberating us from narratives that confine, and for retelling stories that liberate." [260]

Sample Ceremonies and Liturgies

To illustrate how ceremonies and community liturgies can be effective tools for healing, I offer the following examples of ceremonies I've created for groups and individuals:

End-of-Life Ceremony for Alice

Alice developed multiple sclerosis in her early 40s. When I met her in 2012, she was 55, and had been completely paralyzed for several years. In 2018, as her body began shutting down and she began making plans for her death, she asked me to help her create a "letting go" ceremony for herself and her adult children. She had planned her funeral and her cremation, said goodbye to her loved ones, and had a date scheduled to use the assisted death program in her state. But she felt something holding her back.

People were visiting during her last days, and she struggled to converse with them, even though it was exhausting for her. She worried about the grief her children would experience after her exit. All she really wanted to do was gently slip away, but she felt anxious about her emotional ties and perceived obligations. She was ready to go, but did not want to carry that anxiety with her.

Alice was an award-winning horse rider in her youth, and loved all things equestrian. Together (via Skype, since we lived 1000 miles apart), she and I created a "Loosening the Ropes" ceremony, which she performed with the help of her caregiver:

- A table was placed in the middle of the room as an altar. Photos of loved ones, symbols of Alice's accomplishments (equestrian awards, academic degrees, personal objects and other items representing her ties to earth) were placed on the altar.

- On the floor around the altar, her caregiver placed a length of "ranch rope" (the kind used for horses), laid out in a circle around the altar, like a lasso, to symbolize *reining in* and *holding* the objects on the altar.

- One end of rope extended beyond the circle to Alice's bed, where it was tied around her wrist. She could keep it tied there as long as she wished, to represent her sense of being "tied" to her earthly attachments. When she felt ready, she would ask her caregiver to cut it for her. It was a symbolic umbilical cord; just as it was cut when she came into this world, she could now cut it when she felt ready to be born into the next one.

Guilt-Releasing Ceremony for Ramona

Ramona was 65 when her husband died suddenly of a heart attack. They'd had a difficult marriage due to his alcoholism, and Ramona had recently left him and moved to her own apartment...after 40 years together. She was devastated when he died, and tormented by guilt about leaving, berating herself for not having done enough to help him. Her two adult sons, both of whom had recently married and moved to other cities, also felt guilty, feeling that they'd abandoned their father.

Ramona told me about the conversations she had with her sons in which each tried to reassure the other that it wasn't their fault. But despite these reassurances, each of them clung to their guilt. It was as if they were playing a game of "reverse catch," tossing a ball of guilt among them, but instead of wanting the other person to catch it, each person wanted to hold on to it. Nobody wanted to relinquish their guilt.

Ramona lived near the ocean, so I suggested that she and her sons get a beach ball, take it to the beach, and toss it back and forth, with each toss, saying the words, "I release myself from blame and guilt, and I release YOU as well." As the ball gets tossed around, the energy of guilt is loosened and freed, and the family begins to laugh and play. When they feel complete with the process, they take the ball and pop it with a pin, deflating it and releasing the guilt energy.

Letting Go Ceremony for Lacey

Lacey and her husband had moved into a new house. Their old house was now empty, and on the market for sale. The problem was, their ten year-old son, who'd been born in that house, had also died there, from leukemia. Lacey was having a difficult time leaving the house, feeling that it represented an abandonment of her son's memory.

Fortunately, Lacey and I lived in the same town, so I was able to participate in the ceremony with her. We burned sage as we walked room-by-room through the empty house. In each room, Lacey shared a memory of her son. In his bedroom she showed me where he liked to sit on the floor to play with his Legos, and she recalled the many nights she laid beside him in his bed as he suffered through his terrible illness. In the bathroom she fondly recalled his little potty chair from when he was a toddler, and in the kitchen, she talked about the two of them baking cookies together.

In each room, we cleared the memories so that they would not be stuck inside the house, but could go with Lacey wherever she went in the future. Her son had been very artistic, and when she moved, she took all of his drawings with her -- hundreds of them. She knew she didn't want to keep them all, but she couldn't bear to throw them away either. I suggested that she keep the ones she wants, and burn the others in a ceremonial fire in which she could visualize the smoke and heat carrying her love up to her son in heaven.

Community Grief Ritual

In November 2018, with two colleagues, I facilitated a community grief ceremony to support the people and animals who were affected by the wildfires in California.

Each person was given a length of ribbon, and as a group, in silent meditation (with heart-opening music playing), wound the ribbon up into a ball, infusing it with their prayers, their pain, their stories of loss, and their intention for healing.

These "story strings" were then carried, in processional, to an altar made from burnt branches from the areas destroyed by the fires. Each person tied their ribbon onto the branches, allowing their stories and prayers to "unfold" on the altar.

On the altar were also little toy animals to represent the animals who were killed or traumatized in the fires.

After everyone tied their ribbons to the branches, the branches and ribbons were carried outside and placed in a tree, where the stories, prayers and pain could be released to the elements, carried to the divine by the sun, wind and rain.

7

God Needs a New Image

Grieving people often ask me, "Why would God let this terrible thing happen?"

Assuming they are truly seeking an answer (rather than speaking rhetorically), I usually reply, "It depends on what you think God *is*."

Similarly, when someone asks me if I believe in God, I answer with another question…"Which version of god are you referring to?"

During the time I spent as a hospital chaplain, when I'd enter a patient's room and offer a visit, some of them would say, "No thanks. I don't believe in God." And I'd reply, "Good! I don't believe in *that* god either."

In a 2016 article by my friend Bishop John Shelby Spong, he tells a story about his friend Richard Holloway, the presiding bishop of the Scottish Episcopal Church.[261] After giving a lecture, Holloway took questions from the audience, and when an elderly woman asked him, "Do you pray?" he simply said, "No." The audience sat in stunned silence waiting for an explanation.

Holloway allowed them to sit with their discomfort for several seconds before he continued, "Madam, if I had answered your question with a 'yes,' you would have assumed that I accepted your definition of what it means to pray, and your definition of God. That would have been false and misleading, so I had to answer with a 'no.' Now, if we can discuss what we mean by the words "God" and "prayer," and get beyond the confusion between God and Santa Claus, which grew out of our childhood, then my answer might be very different."

This is *exactly* why God needs a new image.

Some people see God as a man-in-the-sky who disburses joy or sorrow, reward or punishment, either randomly or according to what we earn through our behavior. If it's the former -- if our experiences are random and cannot be controlled -- then prayer and religiosity are pointless. If it's the latter, and God is an authoritative parent whose blessings can be earned, then God is essentially running a protection racket. Even if blessings *could* be earned, the rewards are inconsistent and the conditions we must meet to earn them are unclear, which is a very bad form of parenting. When our good behavior isn't rewarded, we feel abandoned, betrayed, terrified and completely alone. With this expectation, despite our efforts to earn the love of this fickle parent, there is no assurance of safety or protection. When the expectation of protection is not met -- and it can *never* be met -- we end up focused more on our feelings of anger and abandonment than on the valuable lessons our painful experiences can teach us.

In John 14:2, Jesus says to his disciples, "In my father's house are many dwelling places." In the world of spirit there are infinite places where consciousness can dwell. The non-physical (spiritual) world is so vast and so beyond our limited understanding that trying to make it fit into a tiny little doctrinal package is just plain foolishness. Paraphrasing something I wrote in *Turning the Corner on Grief Street,* these "dwelling places" are levels of awareness in an ever-expanding network that contains the accumulation of all experience in all of creation. These levels are infinite; they are universes within universes within universes. They cannot be understood in human terms because they exist beyond three-dimensional reality.

Our earthly experiences -- whether joyful or tragic -- are like rooms inside those dwelling places. In fact, they are like dust in the corners of the rooms, or specks in the dust in the corners of the rooms, or cells inside the specks in the dust, which contain a billion more universes within them... and so on forever, beyond physical time and space. When looking at human experience from this vantage point, how could just one system of beliefs explain all that infinite possibility?

My hope is that grievers who struggle to make sense of absurd, unreasonable religious concepts will come to recognize that they're not confined to just one room in the many mansions of theological understanding. Images of God are meant to change as humanity evolves. Stagnation does not serve anyone.

In your own personal moments of theological reflection, I ask you to consider this... is it possible that some things are from God, and others are not? If God is the creator of everything, then all things would have to be from God, including the things that hurt us. If you are someone who believes in Satan, you might say, "All the evil things are from Satan, and the all good things are from God." You might think, as Pat Robertson does,[262] that Hurricane Katrina in 2005 was punishment for America's acceptance of abortion. You might even agree with Jerry Falwell that the U.S. terrorist attack on 9/11 was because of "pagans, abortionists, feminists, gay people and the ACLU."[264]

If you do agree with these things, and if you, as a person of faith, were a victim in one of these events, how would you justify your own suffering? How did you, a pious person, get caught in the crossfire of God's wrath? And how would you explain the suffering of righteous people who've been gunned down in churches, mosques and synagogues by violent extremists...while they were *praying?*

Much of the confusion inherent in religious doctrines could merely be a matter of semantics. Changing our image of God could be as simple as changing the language we use. A Christian's definition of *salvation* might be similar to a Buddhist's definition of *transcendence*. The need for salvation implies that something's wrong; that we are not where we should be, and we need to be rescued by an outside entity. Transcendence suggests that we can view our condition from a higher perspective and heal *ourselves*.

Consider the possibility that there is nothing wrong. Perhaps we are exactly what we should be... an evolving species experiencing all the drama, beauty and intensity of incarnation, which includes both love *and* loss. A spiritual crisis gives us the opportunity to form a new image of God, so why not choose an image based on oneness instead of twoness; an image we can experience as unity rather than separateness? That version of God does not live in a galaxy far, far away. It is not a *being*, and it is not a father, mother, protector or judge. It does not favor one group of people, one nation, or one set of beliefs over another. It is not angry, jealous or violent, nor is it loving, benevolent or forgiving.

It is neutral. Or, as the brilliant rabbi David Cooper said, "God is a *verb*."[265]

Endnotes

INTRODUCTION

1   Laurie A. Burke and Robert A. Neimeyer. "Prospective Risk Factors for Complicated Grief." In Complicated Grief: Scientific Foundations for Health Care Professionals, 2013, Routledge). 154.

2   Melanie E. Brewster, et.al. "Arrantly Absent." The Counseling Psychologist 42, no. 5 (2014): 3.

3   Kim Christian, Samar M. Aoun, and Lauren J. Breen, "How Religious and Spiritual Beliefs Explain Prolonged Grief Disorder Symptoms," Death Studies (May 14, 2018): Published online: 04 Oct 2018. https://doi.org/10.1080/07481187.2018.1469054. 6

4   Jennifer H Wortman and Crystal L. Park. "Religion and Spirituality in Adjustment Following Bereavement: An Integrative Review." (2008. *Death Studies* 32, no. 8). 705

CHAPTER ONE

5   Dixon, D. (2016, December 30). Community & Strength: 10-year-old believes in miracles. Retrieved from https://www.youtube.com/watch?v=Kb20bhgH6TI

6   Christopher G. Ellison, Matt Bradshaw, Nilay Kuyel, and Jack P. Marcum. "Attachment to God, Stressful Life Events, and Changes in Psychological Distress." *Review of Religious Research* 53, no. 4 (2012): 493

7   Terri Daniel, "Grief as a Mystical Journey: Fowler's Stages of Faith Development and Their Relation to Post-Traumatic Growth," Journal of Pastoral Care & Counseling (December 10, 2017).https://journals.sagepub.com/eprint/BTrswSd4UjUssZyJGe4x/full

8   Ibid.

9   James W. Fowler, *Stages of Faith: The Psychology of Human Development and the Quest for Meaning,* 1st edition. (San Francisco: Harper Collins College Div, 1981). 146.

10   "Did God Throw Him Back Down?," *Talk Jesus,* accessed December 8, 2018, https://www.talkjesus.com/threads/did- god-throw-him-back-down.9270/.

11   James W. Fowler, *Stages of Faith: The Psychology of Human Development and the Quest for Meaning,* 1st edition. (San Francisco: Harper Collins College Div, 1981). 153.

12   "Stairway to Heaven: Honoring Dr. James Fowler," Integral Life, April 8, 2009, accessed December 8, 2018, https://integrallife.com/stairway-heaven-honoring-dr-james-fowler/.

13   Ibid.

14   Ibid.

15   Ibid.

16   James W. Fowler, *Stages of Faith: The Psychology of Human Development and the Quest for Meaning,* 1st ed. (San Francisco: Harper Collins College Div, 1981). 146..

17   Terri Daniel, "Grief as a Mystical Journey: Fowler's Stagesof Faith Development and Their Relation to Post-Traumatic Growth," Journal of Pastoral Care & Counseling (December 10, 2017). https://journals.sagepub.com/eprint/BTrswSd4UjUssZyJGe4x/full

18 Daniel Schipani,"The Way, the Truth, and the Life"?: Understanding Healthy & Harmful Spirituality" (Power Point Presentation presented at the Faith and Caregiving Across the Lifespan, San Francisco Theological Seminary, July 13, 2017).

19 Daniel Schipani, "Helpful Interdisciplinary Lenses" (lecture, Faith and Caregiving Over the Lifespan, San Francisco Theological Seminary, San Anselmo, CA. July 2, 2017).

20 Daniel Schipani, "The Way, the Truth, and the Life?" Understanding Healthy & Harmful Spirituality" (Power Point Presentation presented at the Faith and Caregiving Across the Lifespan, San Francisco Theological Seminary, July 13, 2017).

21 Ibid.

22 Ibid.

23 Ibid.

24 "Toxic Spirituality | Dr. David G Benner," accessed July 13, 2017, http://www.drdavidgbenner.ca/toxic-spirituality/.

25 Valerie Tarico and Marlene Winell, "The Sad, Twisted Truth About Conservative Christianity's Effect on the Mind | Salon. Com," Salon.Com, last modified November 1, 2014, accessed December 12, 2018, https://www.salon.com/2014/11/01/the_sad_twisted_truth_about_conservative_christianitys_effect_on_themind_partner/.

26 "The Warning Signs of Toxic Religion," CBN.Com (Beta), last modified September 25, 2013, http://www1.cbn.com/spirituallife/the-warning-signs-of-toxic-religion.

27 David Pakman. "Pat Robertson: Yoga Tricks People Into Speaking 'In Hindu'." YouTube. February 27, 2015. Accessed March 1, 2017. https://www.youtube.com/watch?v=S0j2z4Y6gB8.

[28] Holly Vicente Robaina. "The Truth About Yoga." Today's
      Christian Woman. March 01, 2005. Accessed March 1, 2017.
      http://www.todayschristianwoman.com/articles/2005/march/
      truth-about-yoga.html.

[29] "PraiseMoves | The Christian ALTERNATIVE to Yoga!"
      accessed December 31, 2018, https://praisemoves.com/.

      [30] Ibid.

[31] Rizzuto, Ana-Maria. The Birth of the Living God. Chicago, IL.:
      University of Chicago Press, 1979. 177

[32] John P. Bowlby, *Attachment and Loss*, 2nd Edition. (New York, NY,
      Basic Books,1969), 195

      [33] Ibid, 361.

[34] David A. Cooper, *God Is a Verb: Kabbalah and the Practice of
      Mystical Judaism* (Edition Riverhead Books, 1998). 73

[35] Christopher G. Ellison et al., "Attachment to God, Stressful
      Life Events, and Changes in Psychological Distress.," *Review of
      Religious Research* 53, no. 4 (2012): 495

[36] Matt Bradshaw, Christopher G. Ellison, and Jack P. Marcum,
      "Attachment to God, Images of God, and Psychological Distress
      in a Nationwide Sample of Presbyterians," *The International
      journal for the psychology of religion* 20, no. 2 (2010): 10.

[37] Howard W. Stone and James O. Duke. How to Think
      Theologically (Minneapolis, MN: Fortress Press, 2006). 23.

      [38] Ibid. 2
      [39] Ibid. 20
      [40] Ibid 2
      [41] Ibid. 19
      [42] Ibid. 18

43   Tom Harpur. *The Pagan Christ: Recovering the Lost Light*. New York: Walker &, 2005. Print. 1

44   Terri Daniel. *Embracing Death: A New Look at Grief, Gratitude and God*. Hampshire, UK: OBooks, 2010. 21

45   Jonathan Edwards. "Sinners in the Hands of an Angry God." Internet Christian Library. http://www.iclnet.org/pub/resources/text/history/spurgeon/web/edwards.sinners.html

46   Tom Harpur. *The Pagan Christ: Recovering the Lost Light*. New York: Walker &, 2005. Print. 20

47   Philip Helsel. "God Diagnosed with Bipolar I." *Pastoral Psychology* 58.2 (2009): 183-91. 183

48   Linda Falter. "A Beautiful Anger." *Christianity Today* 55.4 (2011): 34-6. Print. 36

49   Ibid. 34

50   "Camp Fire Death Toll Reaches 86 after Man Dies in Hospital; 3 Remain Missing," *Fresnobee,* accessed December 14, 2018, https://www.fresnobee.com/news/state/california/article222975645.html.

51   "Is California Under a Curse?," *TheTrumpet.Com*, accessed December 14, 2018, https://www.thetrumpet.com/851-is-california-under-a-curse.

52   Mathew Schmalz, "Christian Faith Doesn't Just Say Disasters Are God's Retribution," *The Conversation*, last modified September 6, 2017, accessed December 14, 2018, http://theconversation.com/christian-faith-doesnt-just-say-disasters-are-gods-retribution-83288.

[53] "Anti-Gay Preacher Blames Hurricane Sandy On Homosexuality And Marriage Equality," n.d., accessed December 14, 2018, https://thinkprogress.org/anti-gay-preacher-blames-hurricane-sandy-on-homosexuality-and-marriage-equality-fa202cecf4ac/.

[54] Mathew Schmalz, "Christian Faith Doesn't Just Say Disasters Are God's Retribution," *The Conversation*, last modified September 6, 2017, accessed December 14, 2018, http://theconversation.com/christian-faith-doesnt-just-say-disasters-are-gods-retribution-83288.

[55] Healing from Grief – GriefShare." Accessed December 12, 2018. https://www.griefshare.org/healing/god

[56] Ibid.

[57] Stephen Pattison, Shame: Theory, Therapy, Theology (Cambridge, U.K. ; New York: Cambridge University Press, 2000). 187.

[58] Ibid. 187.

[59] Ibid. 190

[60] William S. Morrow, "Toxic Religion and the Daughters of Job," Studies in Religion/Sciences Religieuses 27, no. 3 (September 1, 1998). 266

[61] Ibid. 264

[62] Ibid. 266.

[63] Ibid. 268.

CHAPTER TWO

[64] Nathan Phelps | *Did Fred Phelps Have a Change of Heart?*, n.d., accessed January 11, 2018, https://www.youtube.com/watch?v=B_4yJSH7Bl8

[65] Avihu Zakai, "The Ideological Context of Sinners in the Hands of an Angry God," *Fides et historia* 36, no. 2 (September 2004): 1–18

66 https://www.ucg.org/bible-study-tools/bible-study-course/ bible-study-course-lesson-4/avoiding-unnecessary-suffering

67 "Poverty Facts and Stats — Global Issues" n.d. http://www.globalissues.org/article/26/poverty-facts-and- stats

68 *The Secret*, 2006, Writer: Rhonda Byrne (original concept). Stars: Bob Proctor, Joe Vitale

69 Ibid.

70 http://www.thelawofattraction.com/what-is-the-law-of- attraction/

71 https://lawofattractionsolutions.com/write-check-make- money/

72 Pema Chodron, *When Things Fall Apart: Heart Advice for Difficult Times* by Pema Chodron (Shambhala, 2005). 61.

73 Kenneth Pargament, "The Many Methods of Religious Coping: Development and Initial Validation of the RCOPE." Journal of Clinical Psychology 56, no. 4 (2000): 519

74 Kenneth I. Pargament et al., "Patterns of Positive and Negative Religious Coping with Major Life Stressors," Journal for the Scientific Study of Religion 37, no. 4 (1998): 711

75 Kenneth I. Pargament et al., "Patterns of Positive and Negative Religious Coping with Major Life Stressors.," Journal for the Scientific Study of Religion 37, no. 4 (1998): 711

76 Ibid. 720

77 Ibid. 721

78 Ibid. 721

79 Stephen Pattison, *Shame: Theory, Therapy, Theology* (Cambridge, U.K. ; New York: Cambridge University Press, 2000). 229

[80] Melissa M. Kelley. *Grief: Contemporary Theory and the Practice of Ministry* (Kindle Locations 622-625). Kindle Edition.

[81] Ibid. Kindle Locations 639-767

[82] Ibid. Kindle Locations 52-57

[83] Ibid Kindle Locations 1174-1182

[84] Ibid. Kindle Locations 832-835

[85] Ibid. Kindle Locations 865-869

[86] Ibid. Kindle Locations 1056-1058

[87] Tom Zuba, "Permission to Mourn." Lecture, Fourth Annual Afterlife Conference, Red Lion Hotel, Portland, OR., June 6, 2014

[88] Scott A. Davison, "Petitionary Prayer," in *The Stanford Encyclopedia of Philosophy,* ed. Edward N. Zalta, Summer 2017. (Metaphysics Research Lab, Stanford University, 2017), accessed December 16, 2018, https://plato.stanford.edu/archives/sum2017/entries/petitionary-prayer/.

[89] "How Are We Like Sheep?," *Christianity.Com,* accessed December 16, 2018, https://www.christianity.com/jesus/following-jesus/discipleship/how-are-we-like-sheep.html.

[90] John Shelby Spong, "Q&A: If God Doesn't Intervene, What Is the Meaning of Intercessory Prayer?" *A New Christianity for a New World*, January 5, 2017.

[91] "Sinners In The Hands Of An Angry God by Jonathan Edwards," accessed December 17, 2018, http://www.iclnet.org/pub/resources/text/history/spurgeon/web/edwards.sinners.html.

[92] C. Douglas Simmons, "Does God Punish Us for Our Sins? - Explore Faith," *ExploringFaith.Org*, accessed December 17, 2018, http://www.explorefaith.org/punish.html.

93 "Suffering—Is It Punishment From God for Sin?," *JW.ORG*, accessed December 17, 2018, https://www.jw.org/en/ publications/magazines/watchtower-no3-2018-sep-oct/is- suffering-punishment-from-god/.

94 Mark Maulding, "Christian Myth #4 - God Punishes Us," *Grace Life International Christian Counseling Center*, May 17, 2017, accessed December 17, 2018, http://www.gracelifeinternational. com/christian-myth-4-god-punishes-us.

95 Do All Suicides Go to Hell? - How Will God Judge Suicides," Bible Knowledge, last modified June 24, 2011, accessed February 6, 2018, https://www.bible-knowledge.com/how-will-god- judge-suicides/.

96 Ibid

97 "Mortal Sin and Hell Question — Apologetics / Moral Theology — Catholic Answers Forums," accessed December 18, 2018, https:// forums.catholic.com/t/mortal-sin-and-hell-question/401598.

98 "40 Sins That Can Send You to Hell," accessed December 18, 2018, http:// peacebyjesus.witnesstoday. org/40SinsThatWillSendYouToHell.html.

99 "List of Mortal Sin | Nigeria Catholic Blog," accessed December 18, 2018, https://catholic-catechism.com.ng/list-of-mortal-sin/.

100 Interview with Fr. Coman Dalton, Telephone Interview, December 18, 2018.

101 John Shelby Spong, *Unbelievable* (New York, NY: HarperOne, 2018). 257.

102 Elizabeth Drescher, *Losing Our Religion: The Spiritual Lives of America's Nones* (New York, NY: Jericho: Oxford University Press, 2016).

103 Kevin Forrester, "How Can Evil Be Explained without Using the Idea of a Real Devil?," *A New Christianity for a New World*, July 27, 2017, accessed July 27, 2017, https://johnshelbyspong. com/2017/07/27/why-im-so-political/?qanda=1.

[104] Terri Daniel and Danny Mandell, *Turning the Corner on Grief Street: Loss and Bereavement as a Journey of Awakening* (First House Press, 2014). 34

[105] Patrick Kelly, "Questions About Trauma And Tragedy As A Test Of Faith," *Find the Power*, last modified 2009, accessed December 28, 2018, http://www.findthepower.com/PageOne/SiteStartQuestionsTraumaAdversityAsATestOfFaith.htm..

[106] Deepak Chopra MD, *Life after Death: The Burden of Proof* (New York: Harmony Books 2006), 75.

[107] Ibid

[108] Jan Brown, "What You Need to Know About New Age Beliefs," *Today's Christian Woman*, accessed February 6, 2018, http://www.todayschristianwoman.com/articles/2001/september/4.52.html.

[109] Chris Lawson, "Potentially Harmful & Dangerous Spiritual Practices - Spiritual Research Network," *Spiritual Research Network*, accessed February 6, 2018, http://www.spiritual- research-network.com/dangerouspractices.html.

[110] Rosilind Jukic, "6 Reasons This Popular Meditation Trend Is Dangerous for Christians," *Charisma News*, accessed February 6, 2018, https://www.charismanews.com/opinion/58612-6-reasons-this-popular-meditation-trend-is-dangerous-for- christians.

[111] Andy Roman, "A Toxic Theology That Emboldens Anarchy | Advent Messenger," last modified May 17, 2017, accessed December 18, 2018, http://adventmessenger.org/a-toxic- theology-that-emboldens-anarchy/.

[112] Elizabeth Kubler-Ross, On Death and Dying (New York: Collier books, 1969). 72

113 Zachary K. Perkins, "4 People Who Successfully Argued With God." *RelevantMagazine.Com,* last modified June 3, 2014, https:// relevantmagazine.com/god/4-people-who-successfully-argued- god.

CHAPTER THREE

114 Maxwell and Perrine, "The Problem of God in the Presence of Grief: Exchanging 'stages' of Healing for 'Trajectories' of Recovery." 179.

115 John Shelby Spong, *Why Christianity Must Change or Die: A Bishop Speaks to Believers In Exile,* Reprint edition. (San Francisco, Calif.: HarperOne, 1999). 59.

116 William James, *The Varieties of Religious Experience* (Seven Treasures Publications, 2009). 182.

117 John Shelby Spong, *Why Christianity Must Change or Die: A Bishop Speaks to Believers In Exile,* Reprint edition. (San Francisco, Calif.: HarperOne, 1999). 61.

118 Marjorie Suchocki, *Divinity & Diversity: A Christian Affirmation of Religious Pluralism* (Nashville, TN: Abingdon Press, 2003), 96.

119 Ronnie Janoff-Bulman, *Shattered Assumptions: Towards a New Psychology of Trauma* — Kindle Edition. Location 149.

120 Ibid. Location 134.

121 Ronnie Janoff-Bulman, *Shattered Assumptions,* First Edition edition. (New York : Toronto : New York: Free Press, 1992). 93.

122 "Seminary Dropout 54: Walter Brueggemann Talking – Reality, Grief, Hope," last modified September 18, 2014, accessed December 14, 2018, http://www.shaneblackshear.com/walterbrueggemann/.

[123] Ronnie Janoff-Bulman, *Shattered Assumptions*, First Edition. (New York: Free Press, 1992), 93

[124] Ibid. 6.

[125] Ibid. 8

[126] John Shelby Spong, *Re-claiming the Bible for a Non-religious World* (Sydney: HarperCollins, 2012), 163.

[127] Ibid. 165.

[128] *Empires, Kingdom of David: Saga Of The Israelites. PBS America,* You Tube, November 23, 2016. Accessed January 26, 2018. https://www.youtube.com/watch?v=leWdKTXiAFk. Part Two: 19:01

[129] Ibid. Part One, 14:28

[130] Ronnie Janoff-Bulman, *Shattered Assumptions*, First Edition. (New York: Free Press, 1992), 9

[131] William S. Morrow, "Toxic Religion and the Daughters of Job," Studies in Religion/Sciences Religieuses 27, no. 3 (September 1, 1998): 276.

[132] Ibid. 273

[133] God on Trial. Directed by Andy De Emmony. Performed by Joseph Muir, Josef Altin, Ashley Artus. BBC Scotland, 2008. https://www.youtube.com/watch?v=5caAug5n8Zk.

[134] Exodus 11:4

[135] Exodus 14:23

[136] *Deuteronomy* 7:1

[137] 1 Samuel 15:10

[138] 2 Samuel 12:15-17

139 God on Trial: The Verdict, n.d., accessed December 10, 2018. https://www.youtube.com/watch?v=dx7irFN2gdI.

140 God on Trial (2008) - Scientist Speech Scene, n.d., accessed December 10, 2018, https://www.youtube.com/watch?v=2eWtrwseINU

141 Frank Rogers. *Practicing Compassion* (Nashville, TN: Upper Room, 2015). 17

142 Richard Elliott Friedman. Who Wrote the Flood Story?. ND. NOVA: The Bible's Buried Secrets. 11 Oct. 2011. http://www.pbs.org/wgbh/nova/bible/flood.html.

143 Roger Isaacs. "Passover In Egypt: Did the Exodus Really Happen?" The Huffington Post. Web. 19 Oct. 2011. <http://www.huffingtonpost.com/roger-isaacs/passover-in-egypt-didthe_b_846337.html>.

144 Richard Elliott Friedman. *Who Wrote the Bible?* San Francisco: Harper, 1997. Print. 138

145 Bob Rosenthal, "Exodus: An Allegorical Portrait of the Human Mind in Its Relationship to God," Tikkun, https://www.tikkun.org/newsite/exodus-an-allegorical-portrait-of-the-human-mind-in-its-relationship-to-god.

146 Louis Dupre, *Light from Light: An Anthology of Christian Mysticism*, ed. James A. Wiseman, 2nd edition. (New York: Paulist Press, 2001). 31

147 Ibid. 33

148 Ibid. 30

CHAPTER FOUR

[149] Mitchell, K. R., & Anderson, H. (2001). All our losses, all our griefs: Resources for pastoral care. Louisville: Westminster John Knox Press. 36-50

[150] Therese A. Rando, *Treatment of Complicated Mourning* (Champaign, IL: Research Press, 1993), 12.

[151] J. William Worden, *Grief Counseling and Grief Therapy: A Handbook for the Mental Health Practitioner*, Third Edition, (New York: Springer Publishing Company, 2001). 89

[152] Ibid. 27

[153] Ibid. 101

[154] Rando, Therese A. *Treatment of Complicated Mourning.* Champaign, IL: Research Press, 1993. 393-448.

[155] Ibid. 648.

[156] Ibid. 453-501.

[157] Conversation with "Richard." Dec. 20, 2017.

[158] Mardi J. Horowitz et al., "Diagnostic Criteria for Complicated Grief Disorder," *FOCUS* 1, no. 3 (July 1, 2003). 904.

[159] Ibid. 909.

[160] Ronald Pies, "The Bereavement Exclusion and DSM-5: An Update and Commentary," *Innovations in Clinical Neuroscience* 11, no. 7–8 (2014). 19.

[161] John Archer. *The Nature of Grief: The Evolution and Psychology of Reactions to Loss* (London: Routledge, 2001). 16

[162] Ibid. 21

[163] Ibid. 23

[164] Laura Matthews and Samuel Marwit. "Complicated Grief and the Trend Toward Cognitive-Behavioral Therapy." *Death Studies* (28, no. 9 November 2004). 852.

[165] Mardi J. Horowitz et al, "Diagnostic Criteria for Complicated Grief Disorder," *FOCUS*. 1, no. 3 (July 1, 2003). 904.

[166] Margaret Stroebe, Henk Schut, "The Dual Process Model of Coping with Bereavement: A Decade On" OMEGA — *Journal of Death and Dying*, Volume 61, Issue # 4 (December 1, 2010). 57.

[167] "The Road to Resilience," www.Apa.Org, accessed January 24, 2018, www.apa.org/helpcenter/road-resilience.aspx

[168] George A. Bonanno, *The Other Side of Sadness: What the New Science of Bereavement Tells Us About Life After Loss*, Reprint edition. (New York: Basic Books, 2010). 98.

[169] George A. Bonanno, "Loss, Trauma, and Human Resilience: Have We Underestimated the Human Capacity to Thrive after Extremely Aversive Events?," *The American Psychologist* 59, no. 1 (January 2004): 20–28.

[170] George A. Bonanno, *The Other Side of Sadness: What the New Science of Bereavement Tells Us About Life After Loss*, Reprint edition. (New York: Basic Books, 2010). 101.

[171] Interview with "Gerald." Telephone interview by author. Sebastopol, CA. 8/20/17

[172] Interview with grief counselor "Robin." In-person interview by author, Sebatopol, CA., 6/10/17

173 Michelle Brown. "Jehovah's Witnesses Use 2,000 Year-Old Rules Regarding Child Sex Abuse, Report Finds." Text. ABC News. (Last modified November 28, 2016. Accessed January 11, 2018). http://www.abc.net.au/news/2016-11-28/jehovahs-witness- handling-of-child-abuse-condemned-in-report/8063798

174 Interview with grief counselor "Robin." In-person interview by author, Sebatopol, CA., 6/10/17

175 Interview with "Donna." Telephone interview by author. Sebastopol, CA. 12/30/17

176 Conversation with "Sam" 4/30/14

177 Interview with "Doug." Email interview by author, Sebastopol, CA. 8/2/18.

178 Interview with "Ursula." Telephone interview by author. Sebastopol, CA. 6/10/18.

CHAPTER FIVE

179 Daniel C. Dennett, *Breaking the Spell: Religion as a Natural Phenomenon*, 1st edition. (Penguin Books, 2006). Kindle location 348.

180 Ibid. Kindle location 362
181 Ibid. Kindle location 403

182 Matthew Fox. *Original Blessing: A Primer in Creation Spirituality: Presented in Four Paths, Twenty-six Themes, and Two Questions* (New York: Jeremy P. Tarcher/Putnam, 2000).

183 Matthew Fox, "95 Theses or Articles of Faith for a Christianity for the Third Millennium," YES! Magazine (n.d.), accessed January 14, 2018, http://www.yesmagazine.org/issues/ spiritual-uprising/1326.

184 Matthew Fox. *Original Blessing: A Primer in Creation Spirituality: Presented in Four Paths, Twenty-six Themes, and Two Questions* (New York: Jeremy P. Tarcher/Putnam, 2000).119.

185 Ibid. 90

186 Ibid. 189

187 Ibid 170

188 Ibid. 222

189 Gregory Anderson *Love, Love, Violence, and the Cross: How the Nonviolent God Saves Us through the Cross of Christ* (Cascade Books, an imprint of Wipf and Stock Publishers, 2010). Kindle location 54.

190 Ibid. Kindle location 57

191 Ibid. Kindle location 808

192 Ibid. Kindle location 1052.

193 Rob Bell, *Love Wins: A Book About Heaven, Hell, and the Fate of Every Person Who Ever Lived*, Reprint edition. (New York: Harper One, 2012).69

194 Ibid. 174

195 Ibid. 178

196 Ibid. 182

197 Gregory Anderson Love, *Love, Violence, and the Cross: How the Nonviolent God Saves Us through the Cross of Christ* (Cascade Books, an imprint of Wipf and Stock Publishers, 2010). Kindle location 292.

198 Roger Wolsey, "Atoning for Bad Theology: Both Kinds.," *Progeressive Christianity*, last modified August 30, 2018, accessed December 21, 2018, https://mailchi.mp/d449f3f9d46c/atoning-for-bad-theology-both-kinds?e=3fa296bb3d.

[199] John Shelby Spong, *Why Christianity Must Change or Die: A Bishop Speaks to Believers In Exile*, Reprint edition. (San Francisco, Calif.: HarperOne, 1999). 83-84

[200] Ibid. 56.

[201] Matthew Fox. *Original Blessing: A Primer in Creation Spirituality: Presented in Four Paths, Twenty-six Themes, and Two Questions* (New York: Jeremy P. Tarcher/Putnam, 2000).90

[202] Linda Mercadante, *Belief Without Borders: Inside the Minds of the Spiritual but Not Religious* (New York: Oxford University Press, 2014), 206

[203] Ibid. 193

[204] Elizabeth Drescher, *Choosing Our Religion: The Spiritual Lives of America's Nones* (New York: Oxford University Press, 2016). 119

[205] Ibid. 189

[206] Benjamin Wormald. "U.S. Public Becoming Less Religious." Pew Research Center's Religion & Public Life Project. November 02, 2015. Accessed March 16, 2017. http://www.pewforum.org/2015/11/03/u-s-public-becoming-less-religious/.207 Harvey Cox. *The Future of Faith* (New York, NY: Harper One, 2009). 5

[207] Harvey Cox. *The Future of Faith* (New York, NY: Harper One, 2009). 5

[208] Ibid. 5

[209] Ibid. 7

[210] Ibid. 9

[211] Ibid. 13

[212] Duane R. Bidwell, *When One Religion Isn't Enough: The Lives of Spiritually Fluid People* (Boston: Beacon Press, 2018). 1

[213] Ibid. 3

[214] Ibid. 46

215 Philip Clayton. *Transforming Christian Theology: For Church and Society.* Seoul: Faith & Intelligence Press, 2012. 112

216 Ibid. 12

217 "America's Changing Religious Landscape | Pew Research Center," May 12, 2015, accessed November 30, 2018, http:// www.pewforum. org/2015/05/12/americas-changing-religious- landscape/.

218 R.D. Putnam and D.E. Campbell, *American Grace: How Religion Divides and Unites Us* (New York: Simon & Schuster, 2010). 159

219 Harvey Cox. *The Future of Faith* (New York, NY: Harper One, 2009). 13

220 Lillian Daniel. *When "Spiritual But Not Religious" is Not Enough: Seeing God in Surprising Places, Even in the Church* (New York, NY: Jericho Books., 2013). 13

221 "4th Principle: A Free and Responsible Search for Truth and Meaning," UUA.Org, last modified September 15, 2014, accessed November 30, 2018, https://www.uua.org/beliefs/what-we- believe/principles/4th.

222 Linda A. Mercadante. *Belief without borders: Inside the minds of the spiritual but not religious* (New York: Oxford University Press, 2014). 192

223 Ibid. 5

224 "Listening to the 'Nones': An Interview with Elizabeth Drescher | Confirm Not Conform," accessed November 30, 2018, http:// www. confirmnotconform.com/blog/listening-nones-interview- elizabeth-drescher.resources/charting-the-new-reformation-part-iii-the-twelve-theses/.

225 "ProgressiveChristianity.Org : Charting the New Reformation: The Twelve Theses," ProgressiveChristianity.Org, n.d., accessed November 30, 2018, https://progressivechristianity.org/ resources/charting-the-new-reformation-part-iii-the-twelve-theses/.

[226] Harvey Cox. *The Future of Faith* (New York, NY: Harper One, 2009). 23

[227] John Shelby Spong. *Why Christianity Must Change or Die: A Bishop Speaks to Believers In Exile* (San New York, NY: Harper Collins, 1999). 47

[228] Galatians 3:28

[229] Lillian Daniel. When *"Spiritual but Not Religious" Is Not Enough: Seeing God in Surprising Places, Even the Church.* (New York, NY: Jericho Books, 2013), 9.

[230] Ibid. 10.

[231] Ibid. 6

[232] Marcia Montenegro, "Comparison Chart of Beliefs," *Christian Answers for the New Age*, last modified 2012, accessed February 7, 2018, http://www.christiananswersforthenewage.org/Articles_ChartBeliefs.html.

[233] Diana Butler Bass, *Christianity after Religion: The End of Church and the Birth of a New Spiritual Awakening* (New York: HarperOne, 2012).

CHAPTER SIX

[234] Eli Holzman, Aaron Saidman, Star Price, *Active Shooter: America Under Fire: Aurora, Colorado*, Documentary (Showtime, 2017).

[235] "The Road to Resilience," www.Apa.Org, accessed January 24, 2018, www.apa.org/helpcenter/road-resilience.aspx

[236] John R. Jordan and Robert A. Neimeyer. "Does Grief Counseling Work?" (2003. Death Studies 27, no. 9: Religion and Philosophy Collection, EBSCOhost). 756

237 Melissa M. Kelley, *Grief: Contemporary Theory and the Practice of Ministry*, 1 edition. (Minneapolis: Fortress Press, 2010).Kindle Location 70.

238 Melissa M. Kelley. *Grief: Contemporary Theory and the Practice of Ministry* (Kindle Locations 70-73).

239 George A. Bonanno, "Loss, Trauma, and Human Resilience: Have We Underestimated the Human Capacity to Thrive after Extremely Aversive Events?," *The American Psychologist* 59, no. 1 (January 2004): 101

240 Colin Murray Parkes, Pittu Laungani, and William Young, eds., *Death and Bereavement Across Cultures: Second Edition*, 2 edition (London : New York: Routledge, 2015). 43

241 Ibid. 223.

242 Ibid. 144.

243 Matthew Fox. *Original Blessing: A Primer in Creation Spirituality: Presented in Four Paths, Twenty-six Themes, and Two Questions* (New York: Jeremy P. Tarcher/Putnam, 2000). 75.

244 Gerald May (2007). Addiction and grace. New York, NY: Harper. 78

245 Kathleen J. Greider (1997). *Reckoning with aggression: Theology, violence, and vitality.* Louisville, KY: John Knox Press. 78

246 Matthew Fox, "95 Theses or Articles of Faith for a Christianity for the Third Millennium," *YES!* Magazine (n.d.), accessed January 14, 2018, http://www.yesmagazine.org/issues/ spiritual-uprising/1326.

247 Ken Doka. "Therapeutic Ritual," *In Techniques of Grief Therapy: Creative Practices for Counseling the Bereaved edited* by Neimeyer, Robert A.(New York: Routledge, 2012). 341

[248] Ken Doka. "Therapeutic Ritual," In *Techniques of Grief Therapy: Creative Practices for Counseling the Bereaved* edited by Neimeyer, Robert A.(New York: Routledge, 2012). 342.

[249] Martín Prechtel, *The Smell of Rain on Dust: Grief and Praise* (Berkeley, California: North Atlantic Books, 2015).

[250] Robert A. Neimeyer. "Therapeutic Ritual," in *Techniques of Grief Therapy: Creative Practices for Counseling the Bereaved* edited by Neimeyer, Robert A.(New York: Routledge, 2012). 274

[251] Todd Hochberg. "Moments Held Documentary" in *Techniques of Grief Therapy: Creative Practices for Counseling the Bereaved* edited by Neimeyer, Robert A. New York: Routledge, 2012. 281

[252] Barbara E. Thompson. "The Commemorative Flag" in *Techniques of Grief Therapy: Creative Practices for Counseling the Bereaved* edited by Neimeyer, Robert A.(New York: Routledge, 2012). 234.

[253] Martín Prechtel, *The Smell of Rain on Dust: Grief and Praise* (Berkeley, California: North Atlantic Books, 2015). 34.

[254] Rando, Therese A. Treatment of Complicated Mourning. Champaign, IL: Research Press, 1995. 395.

[255] Ibid. 395

[256] Ibid. 314-318

[257] Ibid. 393-450

[258] "Grief Rituals," *Spirituality and Grief,* accessed April 1, 2018, http://spiritualityandgrief.com/grief-rituals-.html.

[259] Herbert Anderson. "How Rituals Heal." *Word & World,* Volume 30, Number 1. (Winer 2010). 46.

[260] Ibid. 42.

CHAPTER SEVEN

261 John Shelby Spong, "Progressing Spirit : Charting a New Reformation, Part XXXIII - Thesis #10, Prayer," *Progressing Spirit*, September 1, 2016. https://progressingspirit.com/2016/09/01/charting-a-new-reformation-part-xxxiii-thesis-10-prayer/.

262 "Pat Robertson Says Haiti Paying for 'pact to the Devil' — CNN. Com," accessed March 2, 2019, http://www.cnn.com/2010/ US/01/13/haiti.pat.robertson/index.html.

264 Laurie Goodstein and New York Times, "Falwell: Blame Abortionists, Feminists and Gays," *The Guardian*, September 19, 2001, sec. World news, accessed March 13, 2019, https://www.theguardian.com/world/2001/sep/19/september11.usa9.

265 David A. Cooper,. *God Is a Verb: Kabbalah and the Practice of Mystical Judaism* (Riverhead Books, 1998).

Index

1950s, 94
700 Club, 10

A
Adam And Eve, 21, 89
American Psychological Association, 101
Attachment Figure, 12
Attachment Theory And Images Of God, 11

B
Bargaining With God, 50
Book Of Job, 58–60
Bowlby, 12
Brenner, 9
Buddhism, 25, 28
Buddhist, 94, 112

C
Complicated Grief, i, 33, 75
Counseling, 6, 102

D
Dark Night Of The Soul, 57
Diagnostic And Statistical Manual, 77

E
Exodus, 15, 24, 61, 64–66

F
Facebook, 75
Freud, 12, 78–79

G
God Hates Fags, 23
God On Trial, 61
God Or Godzilla?, 15
Grief Share, 20
Grief Support, 20
Grief Theory, 78
Guilt, 48, 123

H
Heaven vs. Hell, 42
Hell, 45, 48

I
Illusory Transitional Object, 11
Israelites, 17, 24, 41, 55, 58–59, 62, 64

J
James Fowler, i, 2
Jehovah's Witness, 42, 83
Jesus, 13, 16, 21, 23, 36–38, 40, 42, 44, 49, 54, 72, 89–90, 92–94, 96, 99, 110–111
Jonathan Edwards, 16

K
Kyler Bradley, 1

M
Matthew Fox, 87, 92, 108

N
Nathan Phelps, 23
Native American, 38, 89, 106
Natural Disasters, 10, 20, 57,
New Age, 10, 25, 97

P
Pargament, 30
Pat Robertson, 10
Pew Research, 93–94
Positive And Negative Religious Coping, 30
Prayer, 1–2, 30, 38–40, 49, 93, 105

Other Books by Dr. Terri Daniel

A SWAN IN HEAVEN:
Conversations Between Two Worlds

EMBRACING DEATH:
A New Look at Grief, Gratitude and God

TURNING THE CORNER ON GRIEF STREET:
Loss and Bereavement as a Journey of Awakening

CPSIA information can be obtained
at www.ICGtesting.com
Printed in the USA
LVHW012242230122
709142LV00005B/172